Jade Beneath the Sea
—a Diving Adventure

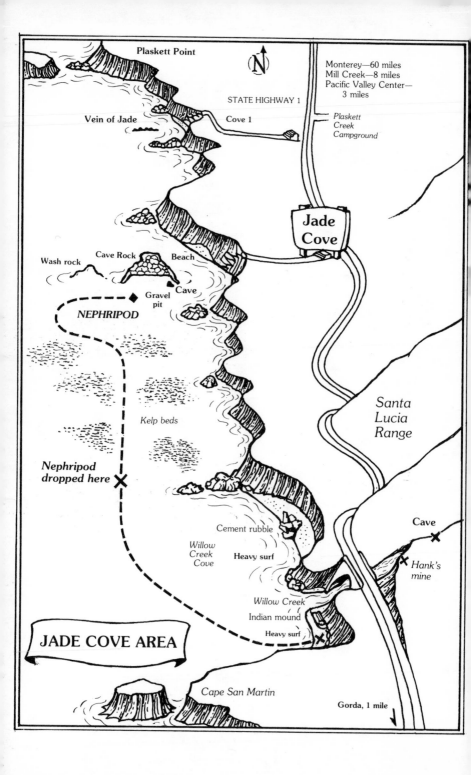

Plaskett Point

N

STATE HIGHWAY 1

Monterey—60 miles
Mill Creek—8 miles
Pacific Valley Center—
3 miles

*Plaskett
Creek
Campground*

Vein of Jade

Cove 1

**Jade
Cove**

Cave Rock   Beach

Wash rock

Cave

Gravel
pit

NEPHRIPOD

*Santa
Lucia
Range*

Kelp beds

*Nephripod
dropped here* ✕

Cave
✕

✕ *Hank's
mine*

Cement rubble

*Willow
Creek
Cove*   **Heavy surf**

Willow Creek

Indian mound

Heavy surf ✕

JADE COVE AREA

Cape San Martin

Gorda, 1 mile

JADE
BENEATH
THE
SEA

A DIVING ADVENTURE

Don Wobber

Pacific Grove, California

Distributed by

Don Wobber
560 Grove Acres
Pacific Grove, CA 93950

(408) 646-9972

Library of Congress Cataloging in Publication Data:
Wobber, Don, 1927-
  Jade beneath the sea.
  1. Treasure-trove—Big Sur, Calif. 2. Jade. 3. Wobber, Don,
1927- 4. Big Sur, Calif. I. Title.
F869.B63W62   917.94'76   75-28279
ISBN: 0-910286-44-2

Printed in U.S.A.

To

Claude

PREFACE

This is my story, a true story with real characters, an adventure I could not help but share. It is the story of a big jade boulder we found in the sea off the Big Sur in California. It has been told in many different ways: in newspapers, in periodicals, in State records, and by word of mouth. From copious notes and tape recordings, I put it down as I saw it before the images blurred. It is a story for divers, for rockhounds, and for adventurers—those who follow their dreams.

If I have done my job well this book should reach out also to those with enough imagination to enjoy vicarious experience. One such was my friend Claude Morris, who was so ill much of his life that he had, more or less, to live the adventures of others. He did thoroughly enjoy mine, and he encouraged me to write this book. I like to think he would have found much pleasure in the final manuscript, had he lived to see it.

I give my hearty thanks to all who are mentioned in the story, especially Gary Carmignani, Sonny Phillips, Ernie Porter, the Moss Landing "gang," and, of course, to Jim Norton. Others unmentioned who helped along the trail were Bud Riggs, Shane Anderson, Ed Stark, "Yip" Yelton, and many more. Thanks also go to the park rangers, and to my professors at the time, Jack Tomlinson and Robert Beeman, for tolerating my missing a few classes and exams.

I want to thank also the many rockhounds and gem and mineral clubs, especially the San Francisco Gem and Mineral Society, for individual and group support. I am grateful to our counsels, and to the many others who gave time and effort freely. For the typing I thank Bytha Morris.

I am especially grateful to Walley Thompson for his considerable work in turning my manuscript into its present form.

Finally, I give warm thanks to my wife, Wanda, who endured and, yes, encouraged me in my quest.

Don Wobber

TABLE OF CONTENTS

I leave Sisyphus at the foot of the mountain! One always finds one's burden again. But Sisyphus teaches the higher fidelity that negates the gods and raises rocks. He too concludes that all is well. This universe henceforth without a master seems to him neither sterile nor futile. Each atom of that stone, each mineral flake of that night-filled mountain, in itself forms a world. The struggle itself toward the heights is enough to fill a man's heart.

One must imagine Sisyphus happy.

—Albert Camus, *The Myth of Sisyphus*

FOREWORD

TARKIN was a mystic, a self-styled "mountain man" with penetrating brown eyes and a full yellow beard. He dressed in a long velvet-green robe with gold trim. He lived with his wife and child in a yellow truck and drove a red Cadillac.

Once Tarkin invited me into his truck to see his jade. In a far corner was a 250-pound boulder, dark green with "flow lines" of lighter green swirling through its surface, deeply sculpted by the sea. He had found it on a remote stretch of California beach. I asked what he planned to do with the jade and he said, dreamily, "I'm just going to let it sit there and watch what goes on around it."

Jade is that way.

Things go on around it.

For

    example,

       take

         a

            certain

              9,000-pound

                jade boulder...

1. THE NEWSPAPER

A ROUGH pebble drops from the cliff to the sea. It turns, reflecting light as it falls through the slanting rays of liquid sun to the depths below. In the timeless sea it is slowly rounded and shaped and finally tossed once again onto the shore. The story of this pebble is our story, for we have returned once again to shore; we have come back different than we were when we entered, and this to us seems important.

August 11, 1971. The newspaper "psshhed" across the driveway like a wave hissing across a gravel beach. Then it stopped and lay there—a white gull, dead on a foreign shore. I lifted it carefully and turned toward the house.

The stars were still out, the air clear and crisp. It would be a good day.

As I entered the house the phone rang. It had to be Jim. No one else would call that early.

It *was* Jim. "Have you read the morning paper?"

"Not yet."

"Well, read it, then call me back. Page six." He sounded worried.

"Bad news?"

"Bad news."

"O.K. I'll call you right back."

I poured some coffee, found page six, and sat down to read. I read it three times.

The headline was plain enough:

STATE AFTER 4 DIVERS WHO FOUND JADE ROCK

The article called us "trespassers" and claimed that our 9,000-pound jade boulder, *The Nephripod,* belonged to the State of California. The meaning gradually came into focus.

Later I stood before the bathroom mirror, gazing at myself. Yesterday a hero, today a thief! My shoulders looked slumped, almost fragile. The grey beard that sprang from my chin was pointed now, like the beard of Mephistopheles.

But wait a minute. We had done nothing wrong. When they hear our side of the story everything will be all right.

1

I was a respected San Francisco businessman just a few short years ago, dressed in a suit and tie, calling on customers on Montgomery Street. Now I inspected my stained white T-shirt ... What trail had I taken since those days that had led to the newspaper's accusations? I searched the article again.

How did I get into this mess?

2. THE COVE

THE STORY might begin anywhere. Perhaps it began in my romance with the sea. From early childhood, like many native San Franciscans, I gravitated to the seashore for the inevitable treasure hunt along the exposed landscape, for the excitement found in a sea shell, in the sudden scuttling escape of a rock crab dropping off a ledge to the safe depths of a tide pool, and in the mysteries of the animals that lived among the bright eel grass.

As a teenager I fished for eels and abalones in the early morning minus-tides at Moss Beach ten miles south of San Francisco, wading up to my waist in the cold water along slippery intertidal reefs, finally driven back by the incoming tide which once again covered the fascinating underwater world. When skindiving became popular it was only natural that I should put on a mask to explore more thoroughly a world I had only glimpsed.

One foggy morning I met a group of abalone divers. They wore gum rubber dry suits to keep warm. Having a mask, snorkle, and fins in the car (I had been diving in Sierra lakes for fishing lures), I joined them and saw my first fish at fish-eye level—a surf perch, glowing in the sunlight like a gold coin against a moving background of emerald-green algae.

From then on I was hooked, and diving became a way of life that will draw me underwater for the rest of my days.

Jade Cove is actually a series of coves located on California Coast Highway 1, 65 miles south of Monterey on the edge of the Los Padres National Forest. This is the isolated, forbidding Big Sur country that Robinson Jeffers populated with characters as rugged as the broken headlands themselves, haunted by the discontented spirits of vanished Indian tribes.

Jade Cove is a rough place to dive. Winter and spring storms out of the northwest drive huge swells directly in from the open sea to pour

over the shallow 30-to-40-foot depths of the cove in powerful ground
swells and breakers. The returning water draining from the coves forms
currents that can sweep an inexperienced swimmer out to sea. Waves
and wind commonly increase without warning in the afternoon. A diver
searching for jade in and among large submerged rocks exposes
himself to constant danger. In the summer the coves are more
protected, but the kelp grows so profusely that by mid-summer a diver

Jade cove, carrying the diving gear down.

cannot get through the tangle on the surface and must either go under
the thickly-matted canopy or use a special float to pull his way over the
thickest places. The diver has to seek places clear of kelp in order to
dive, much as a lake diver in winter might seek a hole in the ice. After
diving in the dim brown light beneath the kelp, the diver returns to his
"hole" and the security of his float to paddle back to the beach.

I first heard of Jade Cove from Perry Yelton, a friend who is an experienced weekend diver. Whenever he spoke of the Cove I grew eager to
see it for myself. Finally, when he thought I had had enough diving experience, he asked if I would like to go diving there with him. Naturally, I
said yes.

We chose a weekend in November, after a series of storms had hit the coast. The land immediately above Jade Cove is a pasture for cattle. We crossed the fence over a stile, then followed a well-worn path through a meadow which tilted toward the sea. My first view of the Cove was from the edge of the 180-foot cliffs which surround it on three sides. I was surprised: it was much smaller than I imagined, and the water was calm and did not look forbidding at all. But, I had never seen such thick extensive kelp beds. We descended the face of the green-black serpentine cliffs by a narrow switchback trail which was blocked in places by recent slides and cut by streams of water from the meadow above, products of an early winter rain. In places the serpentine was as slippery as soap. I fell once, and my gear bag and float jetted into the bushes.

Once we were on the small pebbly beach Perry taught me how to recognize jade. Jade has a soapy feel, he explained, and he showed me that whether the jade is green, black, or some other color, when the surface is moist, being translucent, it appears to glow. The edges do not have a defined appearance but rather a fuzzy look that the experienced hunter can recognize underwater. He pointed out that sometimes the jade is so completely covered with pink or purple encrustations in the form of coralline algae or small animal growth that it can only be seen in small spots where it shows through. If still in doubt, Perry explained, use the end of a rock pick for a hardness test, because jade is harder than steel. He also explained that a pick is useful for digging, prying, and knocking off encrustations.

In a few minutes we suited up and went in.

It is impossible to keep one's eye on another diver when looking for jade. Visibility in the Cove is seldom more than ten feet, the kelp is thick, and the bottom is a maze of large rocks which the diver must continually weave his way through. If he is lucky enough to find a piece of jade, his attention will be on that rock alone, and his partner usually leaves him to continue his own search. If one comes to the surface and the other is digging out a piece of jade wedged between rocks, the diver on the surface may have a long, lonely wait. So I learned to work alone, but I could hear the occasional tap, tap, tap of Perry's rock pick nearby.

While still on my first tank I came across a light green, translucent rock that looked like it weighed about three pounds. Remembering what Perry said, I gave it the hardness test by whacking it several times with the sharp point of my rock pick. Each time the rock failed the test; where the point of the pick made contact a tiny fracture appeared in the otherwise smooth surface.

I hit it once more, inspecting the resulting pin-point fracture. If the rock wasn't jade, what was it? I decided to keep it anyway.

I was at the surface dropping the rock into my gunnysack when Perry surfaced with his hands full of rocks. As he stowed his find in his float I yelled at him, "I found one that doesn't seem to be jade. Can you look at it?"

Perry swam over and looked at the rock. "What do you mean not jade? That's a beautiful piece."

"But it's softer than steel," I argued.

Perry ran the sharp point of his rock pick over its surface. It skidded across without scratching.

"It's jade."

"Oh, is that the way you tell? I thought you whacked it."

"Hey look, you idiot, you whack a diamond with a rock pick and it will fly into a million pieces. You use a scratch test to tell how hard it is. You're not supposed to beat the living hell out of it."

I was learning.

3. JADE FEVER

ON SHORE we compared our treasures. I had found one small, flawless, sea-worn piece, greener than most, with a depression in it that just fit my thumb. I gazed into it, noticing how the milky surface gave way to a deeper green below. I made a special place for it in my pack. At odd times during the day I would look at it, feel it. Rubbing it increased its luster and enhanced its value.

A sea-polished pebble of jade.

Jade, real jade! Maoris, Aztecs, Chinese, Sumerians, Babylonians: back, back into the whorls of prehistory, to the dawn of man. There did not seem to have been a time when jade was not revered as a mystical, religious symbol. And now I had found a very special piece, carved by centuries of sea abrasion, that had taken on a very special meaning for me.

This meaning—the jade, the coast, the sea—became an invisible vortex that slowly tugged at me, pulling at me through feeling and intellect, revealing through my diving some undeniable, deeper, inevitable meaning.

By contrast, the eight-to-five life I led during the week was humdrum, dullsville. I became acutely aware of the frustrations of peddling printing to reluctant customers in San Francisco. As I pounded the pavement in the melancholy shadows of the Financial District, the buildings loomed above like rows of concrete cages. Framed by unscalable walls, the contrasting crisp blue sky, with its white clouds scudding in from the sea, was a mockery to an imprisoned soul. The clouds were free, going somewhere, anywhere, and there I was below, eternally pursuing day after day but always ending in the same place. I needed to escape, no matter for how short a time, into my other world down the coast, to the primitive mountains and the sea. The romance of jade and the mystery of the Big Sur seascape had captivated me.

During the next two years I became obsessed with jade. I wallowed in its history, immersed myself in its mysticism. I cut and polished stones, carved figures, and fabricated jewelry. I dove with a small group of people who were similarly obsessed, and on free weekends and vacations I threw myself into the sea until I was exhausted searching for jade.

We dove Jade Cove in all kinds of weather: blazing sun, thick fog, in wind and pouring rain—even in midwinter, when the Santa Lucia Mountains rising sheer from the sea were capped with snow. I remember heating a jade rock in the campfire, wrapping it in a towel and placing it at the bottom of my sleeping bag to warm my feet until sleep overtook me.

We built a cult of semi-serious superstitions. Certain fish, if followed, led to jade; other fish led away from it. It took a special skill to know which fish to follow. I made a spoon from a solid jade pebble, and each morning before the day's dive I poured myself a jade spoonful of foul-tasting but luck-bringing wheat germ oil. (I generously offered to share this, proclaiming its infallible jade-attracting powers, but seldom got a taker.) For luck we wore jade charms. Each scorned the other's finds, claiming that his own jade was better than all the rest.

We came to know the two accessible coves well. The north cove, Number 1, is narrow and protected. Beneath it running to seaward is a vein of jade which humps up like a green dragon's back through surrounding rock and gravel, disappearing and reappearing for several

The end of the trail for a 90-pound gem.

hundred feet. Black jade, or a mixture of black and green, is found here. Jade is more plentiful in Cove Number 1, but it lacks the quality and color of the jade in Jade Cove, a few hundred yards to the south, where I first dove.

Jade Cove is like home. At the bottom of sheer serpentine cliffs the shore is lined with mammoth piles of stone rubble, with one small break where the stones have been ground into a beach. The stone rubble continues beyond the breakers and out under the sea. It is an endless joy to swim among these familiar rocks and sometimes through long valleys where pebbles and sand gather into gentle ridges, like sand drifts in the desert. On the south side of the Cove shelved ridges of base rock stand up parallel to shore like the tattered backs of sleeping iguanas. Huge boulders dot the Cove, some of them emerging from the water, their craggy shoulders decorated at the waterline with the bright eel grass, pink and dark-purple coralline algae, and blue-black clumps of mussels. Higher up, among patches of white bird guano, the rocks sport an occasional top-knot of brown sea palm. Beneath the water their sides are undercut, and sometimes just above the coarse gravel of the sea floor a surface of slick green jade is revealed, testament to geologic history and millions of years of scouring by the sea.

Eventually, Perry and I decided to take some of the larger jade we had been swimming by for years. There was a reason we couldn't consider bringing out large rocks at the Cove, however. Years ago, when the jade was first discovered, rockhounds came from all over the state to dynamite ledges and hammer large rocks to pieces on the beaches. Trucks and heavy equipment were brought to the edge of the cliffs, and jade boulders were winched up without regard for damage to the trails or the meadow, or, for that matter, the safety of people below. As a result, the U.S. Forestry Service posted signs warning that no vehicles could be used to haul up jade from the Cove.

In our ambitious plans to take large jade rocks we complied with the rules as we understood them. We decided to transport the rocks by floating them to a beach where they could be loaded directly into a vehicle. Because of the prevailing southerly currents there was only one good place nearby, at Willow Creek. While Willow Creek Cove was open to the sea and thus subject to heavy surf, it was only a mile and a half south of Jade Cove, and a road ran right to the beach.

At about this time I met Jim Norton. Jim, who was a rockhound rather than a diver, fit right in. We needed someone with a four-wheel drive vehicle, mechanical ability, and a shop to fabricate specialized equipment. Jim met these requirements and more. He had a cabin at Clear Lake with a garage which harbored a complete workshop with welding facilities. He was a sheet metal man, and handling heavy plates all day had made him as strong as an ox.

In short order the three of us took out several jade boulders. We raised them from the ocean floor by using black rubberized canvas bags, about twice the size of large shopping bags, which we filled with air. When the bags contained enough air to displace the load, the rock with its underwater "parachute" took off for the surface.

The first rock, a 750 pounder, was a near catastrophe. It took us 11 hours to transport it from Jade Cove to Willow Creek. My cousin, there to lend a hand, was appropriately appalled when, at ten o'clock at night, beneath the light of a full moon, we came bolting in through a wild surf at Willow Creek riding the buoyed-up rock on the crest of a wave and heading directly toward a big-as-a-house rock on shore.

"Stop it, you damn fools! You'll kill yourselves!"

We couldn't stop the rock, but we didn't kill ourselves. (The rock now rests in the Oakland Museum. It was a good tax write-off at a time when we were all making money.)

The techniques we learned enabled Jim and me to take an 810-pound rock out in a record time of four hours. By that time Perry was in the hospital with a bad Achilles tendon, which he severed when he misjudged the depth of the water and jumped full force onto a shallow ledge.

Then in 1963 Jim found a 2,400 pound piece. Jim had met another rockhound diver, Ralph Richey, who joined the project along with a couple of his friends. After much frustration and not a little drama, we finally beached the large gem.

These group jade recovery efforts were both work and fun, with a sense of excitement and camaraderie I had never found in the business world. I had vague dreams of one day being a part of a group that would get a really large rock, maybe, say, as big as a canoe.... I had visions of paddling this "jade canoe" down to Willow Creek, but I had no idea that these visions would ever materialize.

4. NEW BEGINNINGS

DURING the twenty-plus years of my early diving experience I was in the printing business with my brother in San Francisco. During a period when our company was prosperous I had an opportunity to sell my share of what had been a three-generation family business. By that time my two sons were off at college and my wife had gone back to college to pursue a career in psychology. Because my sons were not interested in

Lifting a 175-pound rock. Clipping a lifting bag to the net.
Filling the lifting bag with air from the diver's regulator.

Bag filled, the rock is ready to go to the surface.
Swimming the raised rock to the beach.

the printing business and I felt dissatisfied with the world of suits and polished shoes, my wife and I decided that it was time to make a second start—only this time I was going to choose a career that more closely matched my interests. For twenty years I had been like a pebble pushed back and forth in the shallows; now I wanted my future to reveal a deeper wearing, the shape of a more meaningful life. No more business conferences into the wee hours, no more nights spent restlessly tossing, mulling over union negotiations, production, collections, accounting. I wanted a life I could control with my own two hands. With the blessings of my family, I sold out and cut loose.

Suddenly free at the age of 44, I decided to go back to school, convinced that somehow my new life would have to tie in with the sea.

5. A PROJECT

AT SAN FRANCISCO State University I found a good working-diving group of marine biologists. We dove often and grew to be close friends.

One of my new diving companions was Gary Carmignani. At 27 Gary was an easy-going, swinging, bachelor type. Tired of being a stock broker, he had decided to go back to school and was finishing work toward his master's degree: a study of the effects of pollution on the shell growth of bay mussels. I envied his free, relaxed, breezy manner— and the fact that he had no more classes to suffer through. As my unofficial advisor he showed me how to procure materials from the stockroom for my projects without going through the usual time-consuming red tape. Just watching Gary put me in good spirits. Everything was so easy for him, whereas I tended to worry things through. He shuffled through the halls in broken-down moccasins, as if he were scooting along on two small, completely unattached barges. He had classic Roman features, but below his neck his body almost seemed to be a foreign appendage. Often he appeared not to know what to do with his arms, which hung loose in their sockets from broad shoulders. He had a certain little-boy naivete, a certain surprise at life, like a flower opening one morning and discovering, "Oh, I'm a flower!" Once he confided to me, "I think I'm 20 years immature." Perhaps that is the secret of a truly free spirit.

On a three-day weekend during the winter semester, my new diving companions and I organized an expedition to Jade Cove, where we were going to survey for jade. I suggested an area around Wash Rock in the center of the Cove, where we worked at a depth of 40 feet at the rock's base. We used ropes marked off in meters, running a grid pattern by compass across the bottom. The plan was to use biological study-plot techniques and to map the exact location of all the jade we found on plastic writing boards. Our efforts were fruitless, however, because we found no jade, not even a pebble.

The next day the scientific method was abandoned—and we had more success. When we later compared our treasures on the shore we saw that Gary had found the best pieces of jade. In only a short time he had also become afflicted with jade fever.

Gary and I were the last divers out of the water that day. At the top of the trail we threw down our gear and lay on the grass overlooking the slate-grey sea. The sun dissolved behind a solid bank of fog.

I told Gary about how I had taken a film-making course and was putting together underwater movies, and about how I wanted to shoot a film on jade. I wanted to capture the thrill of finding a beautiful, fist-sized jade rock; the exciting race to the surface, treasure in hand; a close-up of the diver looking at the jade on the way up, and the way the colors change when the light-filtering qualities of the water decrease as the diver ascends. I wanted the audience to feel the excitement of raising larger rocks—of discovering them, digging them out and rolling them into nets, of sending the jade on its way to the surface. I wanted my film to capture a sense of the history of jade, of its power and the magic spell it has cast over people throughout the ages.

We looked down at the ragged green serpentine cliffs and watched the tide slowly recapturing the beach as we talked about making a film. As my excitement mounted so did Gary's enthusiasm.

"I'll be finished with my master's by midwinter, and I'll have the next six months free," Gary said. "I could camp at the Cove and dive for jade, then call you when the water looks good."

"I could come down on weekends and vacations to film," I added.

After dinner our group sat around a campfire, drinking wine and swapping stories. I took Gary aside.

"Gary, if you're really serious about coming down, we could film raising a big rock. We could get some footage of finding the rock and the whole process of raising it to the surface. Then we could tow it to Willow Creek and shoot bringing the rock in through the surf."

Gary agreed that we could probably get some exciting footage.

The following three days I thought about my talk with Gary. I wasn't sure I wanted to get involved in another project at that time. After all, I had just made new commitments to my studies and a new career. Making the film shouldn't be just another form of escape. But I would only be working with Gary on weekends and during school breaks, I rationalized; and all extended filming would be done during Easter vacation or in June when school was out. And the break from studies would be good for me.

I had recently become aware that the things I considered important often reflected some childhood interest, as though life was mysteriously drawing me back, returning me to an earlier time. Wish-fulfillment, repetition-compulsion—it was all very Freudian. Perhaps what I was involved in at this stage of the game was a semiconscious search for meaning, for identity. As a child in his search to become himself defies parental rule in order to do things in his own way, so in returning to school I was defying convention to seek my own meanings. But I was really seeking those things important to me, a belated search for my own self, a person I had not been able to reach in many years.

I began to fit the pieces together. My love of animals might be traced to the love of playing with live or stuffed animals in a childhood world of invention and imagination. Now, through marine behavior studies, hadn't I sought out the same sort of animal-filled world? New skills and maturity had been brought to bear on old desires—and now I returned not only to my animals but also to my second childhood love, rock collecting. Here too I found an unfulfilled need for identity long buried, a need to do something myself, in my own way. My childhood rock collecting had been terminated unwittingly by the misguided generosity of my grandfather, who, on my ninth birthday, presented me with an exotic collection of mineral specimens from all over the world. How could he have guessed that from the moment I received that over-whelming collection until I first climbed down the cliffs at Jade Cove as an adult I would not collect another rock? My need was to collect at my own pace, to live my own life and be allowed to discover things for myself.

Once I had worked out this rationale for the rock-collecting-filming project that I emotionally wanted to do anyway, I began to think on more detailed, practical levels.

In order to film the raising of a big jade rock we would need Jim Norton. We also needed another filmmaker as a fourth member, someone who could work with Jim and Gary when I wasn't available. He should be a student, preferably a diver—someone with time on his hands who would be willing to work without pay.

I took Gary to meet Jim. On the way to Jim's house I tried to describe Jim, who is not a simple man to describe. There is something unique about him, an almost religious sense of obligation to others. You have no doubt at any time where he is in regard to you; you know he will give one-hundred percent of himself.

Thirty years of sheet metal work have made Jim strong and muscular. His hands are thick and scarred from years of hard labor, hands like weapons that could be used for peace or war, hands that play the violin and that nearly put a man out forever in a street fight. Rough, gentlemanly, unpolished, sensitive, wild, stubborn—Jim was a man you could always count on.

Jim liked our idea. To him it meant not only a new adventure but also the possible fulfillment of his ten-year-old dream to get the biggest jade rock ever to come out of the ocean.

We lined up a cinematographer. Now all we needed was a rock.

6. TO FIND A ROCK

THE CINEMATOGRAPHER, who had a busy schedule, said he would come down to the Big Sur country after we had chosen a rock. We were in no hurry. Since time was no problem, we felt it would be wise to consider several large rocks, measure them, and then choose the best one.

For starters, I knew of two rocks in Jade Cove. One, about 800 yards offshore in 40 feet of water, was cylindrical in shape, five feet high by six feet wide. There was a fracture near the base, which was buried in the sand, where it might break off. One section, halfway up, was bright green where it almost touched a huge jade rock that ran to within three feet of the water's surface. The larger rock, so big that we could not consider it, had a brilliant patch of jade facing the smaller rock, and the two jade surfaces reflected bright green off one another. I imagined filming a diver's face between these jade surfaces, green reflecting from both sides. But after inspecting all sides of the rock we decided that it wasn't quality jade throughout, and also that it wasn't a good shape.

The second rock we looked at was closer in, about 300 yards directly west of the beach in 35 feet of water. Since it was in an area commonly worked by divers, it had become an underwater landmark over the years. I had seen it often during the past 15 years but had never really considered trying to bring it in. It was about seven feet long by three feet wide by six feet deep. The exposed side looked good, but the rest of the rock was hidden under an enormous ledge.

Both of these rocks were possibilities. However, when we calculated their weight we found that the first one weighed about 15,000 pounds and the other 6,000 to 7,000 pounds. Both were too heavy for what we had in mind. A 4,000-pound rock would be about right.

We decided to explore other areas to find the right rock, since jade had been found from Plaskett Rock, a half-mile north of the Cove, to below Gorda, a service-station grocery-store town two-and-a-half miles south. At the south end of the Willow Creek beach there are deposits of grape or bubble jade, technically called *botryoidal*. This is one of the few places in the world (some say the *only* place) where bubbly-surfaced jade is found. Such pieces have been worn smooth by the sea, and what were once bubbles are now whirlpool-like patterns of color. Essentially, most of the coastline underwater was unexplored.

We bought a small inflatable rubber boat called a "Speedyak," which we fitted out with Jim's 3.5 h.p. Elgin motor. Gary's father let us use his old life raft. I had some lifting bags left from former jade expeditions. I repaired the holes in them and began scouting surplus-stores for more.

Rumors of a surplus auction at the Naval Air Station sent Jim and me to Alameda, across the bay from San Francisco. To our surprise, we found a whole pallet of lifting bags, perhaps a hundred of them, all in good shape. Each bag was capable of lifting 175 to 200 pounds; altogether they could lift a minimum of 17,500 pounds! We bid $34 for the lot, but it went for $60.

After the auction we located the buyer and offered him $60 for half of the bags. He agreed, and we were in business. We picked up grommeting equipment, 60 clips, and some nylon line, and modified the bags.

The following week we were back at the Cove. We inspected the two rocks again and decided that the smaller one, the one closest to shore, was more suitable. Using a meter stick (weighted so that if we let go it would not float to the surface) and a plastic writing board with pencils tied to it, we sketched the jade boulder and the rocks surrounding it. Jim and I measured while Gary wrote down figures. We found the rock was eight feet long, five-and-a-half feet wide and three-and-a-half feet high! Since light refraction causes underwater objects to appear one-third larger than they actually are, you can imagine how big it looked to us.

Most of the jade rock was wedged in tight under an overhanging ledge formed by an undercut in a house-sized rock that emerged about 15 feet above the surface of the water to form a small 30 x 30 foot island. We named the island the Cave Rock because it has a cave through its base on the shoreward side. The overhanging ledge came to within an inch of touching the jade rock, and a 300-pound rock was wedged between them.

The next day we decided to search a different locality. We went 10 miles north to Mill Creek, where a deep draw opens onto a beach. We launched our motorized Speedyak and Jim pulled Gary and me in the raft. We headed south toward Plaskett Rock, a large offshore sea stack.

Jim comes up the trail, Plaskett Rock in the background.

I was excited about checking out this area, since I had heard stories about jade from there for several years. By the time we got to our destination Gary's father's raft had begun to leak. I circled Plaskett Rock underwater, hoping to mark jade indications as I swam, while Gary, whose regulator was not functioning, stayed in the leaking raft and bailed. I circled, exploring the whole circumference of Plaskett, but found no signs of jade.

When I came up Jim cut the raft loose with Gary and me on it, so he could look for a shorter way back. He took the Speedyak into the Cove to see if the kelp was sparse enough to get through. Then the starter rope on the outboard broke and he started to paddle back to us. We could just make him out in the distance. We began paddling toward him, our sinking raft dangerously low now in the dense kelp. Bailing and paddling, we made little progress. When Jim got close he stayed outside the kelp bed and tossed us a line. To help, I got in the water and pushed. Finally, by pushing and pulling, we made it into an open channel, and Jim opened the outboard motor and cut and attached a new starter rope.

I strapped on a second air tank and scanned the sea floor all the way back to Jade Cove while Jim towed the raft, following my air bubbles from above. I found no jade, large or small.

The next day Jim was planning to leave by noon, so Gary and I dumped a tank apiece in the Speedyak to try our luck off the cliffs below Gorda. We had just rounded Cape San Martin, at the south end of Willow Creek Beach, when the motor conked out, so we paddled to the closest cove. Again no jade. When we got aboard the Speedyak again we discovered that the oars had fallen overboard and drifted away. Jim appeared at the top of the cliff to say good-by, then came down to try to start the motor. But even his mechanical genius failed to breathe life into it. He finally had to leave, and we paddled back to Jade Cove, using our swim fins for oars.

Gary and I had an early dinner and polished off a bottle of Red Mountain wine. After dinner I sat in the sun on a large rock facing the creek, watching seagulls bathe and preen in the sweet-water where the creek joins the sea. The gulls, in from a day's foraging, were now content to squawk quietly at each other, once in awhile joined by latecomers. I enjoyed watching the gulls in flight. Often at my desk at home, neglecting homework, I had gazed dreamily out the window at the beautiful white and grey birds circling ever higher against the sky, challenging the west wind. Now, warm with wine as I sat on the rock at Willow Creek I saw a single naked, shining bird piercing the sky with its being, proclaiming its existence, its dominion in space and time. It was living a life that was all-consuming—and certainly more real than mine. I longed to be truly myself, to be free of obligation, even of goals—free enough to listen to the rolling of a wider sea, both within and without, that glistens white and wild from horizon to horizon.

Suddenly the gulls rose in unison. Around the north cliff came Tarkin, a local character whom I had seen before only from a distance as he searched the beaches. He came toward me, wading through the creek. He was the local primitive, a sort of guru—tall, slender, with long, matted blond hair and beard, wearing knee-high boots.

I stood up. "Did you find anything?"

"See this jewel?" His long, slender fingers suspended a slim pebble of jade in front of the fading sun. The jade was round, about the size of a silver dollar but twice as thick at the center, its edges smoothly rounded as if ground and polished on a lapidary wheel. The sunlight shining through it transfixed me. The deep blue-green glow of the center feathered out to a brightly lit circumference. It was a luminous planet, suspended in space.

Tarkin smelled unpleasant, the musky smell of a thousand years. Somehow, in or around him a heavy distant thunder seemed to echo. His dark eyes, hard to meet, seemed to lay me bare, as if they reflected some primitive, unthinkable past. They held a revulsion-attraction in which was embodied all the mystery of antiquity—something I did not want to look at, like some heinous primitive religious rite. And yet he was just a man. Words seemed to be inadequate, unnecessary with him.

He ran the stone along both sides of his nose, grease-coating the surface, then dropped it in my hand. As I tilted the stone my image was clearly mirrored back to me in its luster.

"Fantastic!"

"I've been trying to pick up this piece for five years," he said.

I returned it to him. He clenched it in his hand and walked away.

The following morning I dove to have another look at the rock under the ledge in Jade Cove, taking along an underwater lamp. The whole visible side of the rock was bright green and, although about half the surface was covered with coralline algae and sponges, wherever I scraped with a knife the jade beneath was good. I swam to the top edge, peering down into the darkness between the ledge and the Cave Rock, then turned on my lamp and gasped. The far side of the jade rock rolled down in smooth ridges of brilliant green where the jade had been sand abraided and polished like a jewel! I tried every way I could to wedge myself in farther for a better look, but I soon realized that I would have to be satisfied with only a glimpse. It was the finest jade rock I had ever seen—one hell of a jade canoe!

Later, Jim, Gary, and I calculated the size and weight of the rock more precisely. I figured it at 7, 929 pounds, which roughly agreed with Jim's calculations. Even though it was much larger than I had wanted to try for, I found that I had fallen in love with it—good God, what a gem!

We all agreed that this was the rock we wanted to take. Once we agreed on it our decision seemed irreversible. There was no need to look any further.

Jim christened it the "Nephripod," since he said that it was a pod of nephrite jade. A silly name, I thought, but what the hell?

7. MASTER PLAN

NOW THAT we knew the Nephripod's weight, size, and shape we decided to sketch a scale model of it. Like a magician, Jim came up with a pad of yellow construction paper on which he had already made detailed drawings of a trailer massive enough to haul the rock. Jim's four-wheel drive Ford Bronco with its oversized tires for traction would pull the trailer. Gary and I were amazed as we pored over the elaborate drawings that Jim had done already—even before we had agreed on that particular rock.

Jim had the above-water technical problems solved; but he was not a diver, and there would be terrific problems underwater—problems that he couldn't foresee. I knew it was too late, however, because I knew how stubborn he was. I was still afraid of getting into a situation we couldn't back out of. It was one thing to agree to try for something for fun but another to dedicate yourself to it completely, as he was doing.

"Let's keep an open mind in case we can't loosen the rock," I argued, "This is supposed to be a film, not a goddam Federal Project."

But I saw it was hopeless; Jim was beyond all compromise.

As he described the equipment he was in seventh heaven, but to us he was talking a foreign language. Jim had a reputation for equipment overkill. When he built things they were stronger, heavier, and assembled in a far more complex manner than was necessary. He insisted on doing things the "right way"—which also meant the hard way and the expensive way. He wanted to build the trailer from scratch. From the looks of his plans this was his finest hour!

With sinking heart, I studied his diagrams of electric brakes and other wiring. Let him build the damn thing any way he wants, I thought; he will anyway. In the meantime Gary and I will have plenty to keep us busy at the bottom of the ocean.

"O.K., Jim, O.K. A six-wheel trailer with electric breakaway gear ... I guess you know what you're doing."

Jim was going on a mile a minute. "Well, if the hitch breaks and the trailer gets loose, that's 8,000 pounds of jade and 1,500 pounds of trailer hurtling down the highway. With break-away brakes it stops right now, and *automatically.*"

I broke into a cold sweat as I envisioned an island of jade on a trailer screeching to a sudden halt in rush-hour traffic in the middle of Bay-shore Freeway.

"We can also use the trailer to display the rock. We can paint it with bright colors and haul it to rock shows," he added, looking directly at me with a visionary sparkle in his eyes.

"Can the Bronco haul it? It seems awfully small."

"It has the power, but we may need help coming up the grade out of Willow Creek. I'm worried about that. I don't know about that steep grade. We may need a tow truck." He had thought of every detail.

"O.K., O.K.," I replied. "Once it's on shore, Jim, the *Nephripod's* your baby. All I'm concerned with is the underwater part."

"Look." Jim shoved another drawing at me. "I've designed a sled. Under the water the jade can be muscled onto the sled. The sled has pipes under it; they're part of the frame. We can put chain through them, pull the chain up over the rock and tighten it with load binders. Then we can run chain from the ends of the sled, where I'll weld hooks. We'll put clevises on to join the chain together where it crosses...."

"A chain net over the rock?" I liked the idea.

"A chain net, and held in place with shackles. And we can hook the lifting bags to the chain links wherever we want. Put barrels around for additional lift. Once we get our rock on the beach the chain threaded through the pipe can be used to pull the sled. The sled will slide across the beach and over boulders."

Gary was sitting silently, his mouth open. Miraculously, Jim had us out of the water with that rock again.

I looked at another list Jim had written, entitled "RECOVERY PRO-
CEDURE"—something to do with lowering barrels to the bottom.

**Detach one barrel and insert male fitting in chuck to flood barrel.
Have line on sled to guide in position. Lead line from sled through
pulley on rock and stand clear on bottom....**

My head was spinning. This was too complicated a thing to do in *my*
ocean, but there was no stopping Jim now. Sure, I'd go along with him,
but, damn it, I would do things my own way underwater.

We let Jim have his way in building his trailer, but what the logic was,
or whether there was any logic at all, I can't recall. We were captivated
by that awesome rock, and we went ahead as though all obstacles
would be overcome, no matter what they might be. It wasn't logical, but
logic didn't matter. We had the fever!

8. THE WEDGE

A SERIES of early winter storms struck the coast, each one tailing
another. Small-craft warnings went up and stayed up for weeks.

Jim was at his cabin at Clear Lake, industriously assembling the sled
and the jade trailer in his garage, so one weekend I went up to help. He
had gear spread out all over the garage, happy as a clam. Among other
things were six empty 50-gallon steel drums, which had last been filled
with epoxy resin. I drained and cleaned them and Jim showed me how
to cut metal strips to form three hoops around the circumference of the
barrels. One in the center and one at each end. As I worked on the
hoops Jim welded large plates to a framework of pipe. This was to be
the sled, which would slide up a steel ramp onto the trailer.

Jim had purchased a griphoist, a device for gaining a mechanical
advantage, which was to be used as a primary tool underwater. It is a
slim metal box, rounded at the corners, with a hook at each end and
two knobs with which to attach an expandable handle: one knob to
move cable through a hole through the box in one direction, the other
to move it in the opposite direction. It has a clutch and when it is in
neutral the cable pulls freely in either direction.

To test the griphoist I looped some chain around a large granite rock
in the driveway, attached a snatch block (a pulley device) to the chain,
then wrapped another long length of chain around two trees about 30

feet away. One griphoist hook was put through the chain on the trees, and the opposite hook attached to an eye on the end of a long steel cable. The cable was run out through the snatch block and back through the hole in the center of the griphoist. I fit the expandable handle to one of the two knobs on the griphoist and pumped back and forth. With each pump the cable was pulled through the hole an inch, gradually putting tension on it. The rock weighed about 500 pounds. It was easily dragged across the driveway.

That night Jim and I discussed how much jade a single lifting bag could take to the surface of the water. We figured the specific gravity of jade, then filled a lifting bag with water to check its volume, then figured the displacement in salt water. We came up with different figures, Jim's much lower than mine. In such disputes over mechanical technicalities, Jim, with his practical experience, had the advantage. I called him the "stubbornest man in the world," and he said I thought he was stubborn only because I was so bullheaded that no one else would argue with me. But we both realized the importance of knowing how much jade a bag would lift, so I said I would check the actual lift power in my uncle's swimming pool.

Later, back in the Bay Area, Gary helped set up the test. My uncle's pool was as cold as ice, but when we were finished with the test my aunt warmed us up with a glass of brandy.

That night I telephoned Jim to report that a bag could lift 175 to 200 pounds of jade—just what I had figured.

He was skeptical. "What kind of jade did you try to lift?" he asked testily.

"Oh, just some old crap I had around the house."

Jim said that my test wasn't accurate, since good jade weighs more than crappy jade. He carried on like that, defensively.

That was too much! I got back into my diving gear right then, took all my best jade, and went back to my uncle's pool. I weighed out 185 pounds of jade, put it in a net and threw it in the pool. Then I put on my tank, went down to the bottom of the pool, attached a lifting bag to the net and breathed air into the bag. The bag carried the jade to the top easily and when it was floating four inches of bag showed above the surface.

"Besides," I told Jim triumphantly when I talked to him again, "the bags will have even more lift in salt water."

He still wasn't convinced.

When the weather cleared up we took Jim's 15-foot house trailer down the Big Sur, to the Plaskett Creek Campground, over a four-day weekend. The house trailer had butane lamps, a stove and an oven, a sink, and storage space. When the two bunks were folded back there was a table which could seat up to six people. It was compact, but we felt as if we were living in luxury.

We decided that it would be wise to keep the real nature of our project secret, even from our closest friends. If people got curious, especially other divers, we told them we were working on a rock that weighed only about 3,000 pounds. This ploy was to discourage talk among other divers, especially dive clubs and organized groups, and to avoid getting local people and tourists too interested. We were afraid that if attention should be drawn to the rock other divers might try to take chips from it, or might take some of the equipment we stored underwater. Or once we had our gear ready to raise the rock to the surface, they might even try to pirate it from us. Besides, we might not get the rock, and 8,000 pounds is a hell of a lot of egg to clean off your face—even when split four ways.

On this trip we brought the griphoist, chain, cable, crowbars, and other miscellaneous gear. We brought as many air tanks as we could, because the nearest place we could fill them was Cayucos, 45 miles to the south. I had four sets of double tanks and Jim had a double and two singles. We rented and borrowed others and even bought three new 100-cubic-foot tanks.

I had made another float, which we used to transport gear between shore and the dive site. It was made of an eight-inch diameter styrofoam log bent into an elongated horseshoe shape around a fiberglass board, with a pocket at the front end for gear. The diver lay on the board, his legs between the styrofoam logs, and kicked for propulsion. While this float became a workhorse, like much of our experimental equipment it was another "back-to-the-drawing-board design." It was all right until the diver pulled himself up onto it, but then, since it wasn't bouyant enough, the seawater rushed in and filled the front pocket, making it too heavy. As we worked with it, it gradually disintegrated, so that we thought each dive would be its last.

Our cinematographer partner had to leave us, so there were only the three of us, Jim, Gary, and me. The burden of photography now lay in my hands, since Gary was in poor shape, capable of only one or two tanks a day, and Jim's diving was limited because he not only got seasick but his ears hurt from pressure changes, even at 35 feet. (Some-times Jim would admit this and sometimes he wouldn't, but he always carried his tanks down the cliff with all good intentions. Then, since I love diving, I would often use Jim's tanks and mine too.) Even though Jim was able to dive only a few times, however, he took the best under-water footage we have.

During our four-day weekend the water in Jade Cove was relatively calm. We decided to concentrate on removing the rock that was wedged between the *Nephripod* and the overhanging ledge of the Cave Rock. We had already tried to loosen it by hitting it with a sledge hammer and prying it with crowbars but had only managed to move it slightly.

We paddled our cables, chain, griphoist, and other equipment out in the float and dropped them near the *Nephripod*. Then we dove. First we tied a heavy nylon rope around several large submerged rocks about forty feet to the shoreward of the *Nephripod*. We hooked the griphoist to the rope, tied chain around the protruding end of the Wedge Rock, and hooked a snatch block to the chain. We ran the cable through the snatch block and back through the griphoist.

Jim was worried that the huge ledge overhanging the *Nephripod* might drop either on the *Nephripod* or on us when the Wedge Rock was pulled out. A point of contention.

Since the water was clear, I readied my 16 mm camera and a Super-8 Nizo time-lapse camera. I had plans to shoot the removal of the Wedge Rock in time-lapse photography, letting the Nizo run by itself while shooting at normal speed with the 16 mm. I screwed the Nizo tightly to the tripod, and since a surge was running, caused by passing swells overhead, I started to pile rocks against the tripod legs. As soon as one leg was wedged in the other two would lift with the surge. Finally, all of them were solidly covered with rocks. I turned the camera on and through the housing could hear it running. I went to help the others, pleased that I would be in the movie too.

Five minutes later I returned and found the camera facing in the wrong direction. A surge had loosened it from the tripod. I screwed it back on, tightening it hard. As I resettled it a large surge swept past, sending a shower of sand, gravel, and seaweed debris off the bottom and knocking over the camera, the tripod, and me. I tried once more and failed again. In disgust, I unscrewed the time-lapse camera and swam with it up to the float. Father Neptune now has a tripod, and he's welcome to it! I had more success with the 16 mm camera. I swam through the cave that runs through the Cave Rock, filming as I went. The cave is actually formed by two or three rocks leaning against one another, all of which have one thing in common: they are solid jade on their lower surfaces. An opening at each end permits a diver to swim in one end and out the other. Inside, on the ocean side, is a five-by-eight-foot wall of some of the most beautiful jade in the Cove, the surface solid, smooth, without a fracture—to me one of the unsung wonders of the world!

The south entrance of the cave leads to the Gravel Pit, a 20 by 40 yard area alongside the Cave Rock covered with small- to fist-sized gravel. A swim through the cave to the Gravel Pit and a seaward turn through the Gravel Pit about 20 yards takes you directly to the *Nephripod*. The Gravel Pit is subject to heavy surges caused by the flow of water washing around the Cave Rock and thus is usually stirred up, so that small pieces of jade are continually being exposed.

When I started to film Gary he was tightening the cable. While he was being filmed he was supposed to give the appearance of doing difficult, serious work—but there he was, sleeves unzipped and rolled back, a wisp of black hair rakishly flapping from under his hood like a puppy dog's tail. To top it off, he was pumping the griphoist with only one hand. The other one was on his hip, making him look as if he were doing a folk dance.

I burst out laughing. I laughed so hard that I had to go to the surface and drag myself out on a rock to recover.

We continued to work on the Wedge Rock. At first we applied too much pressure and sheared off the pins inside the griphoist. We unhooked the griphoist and took it to shore for repairs (we thought we had broken it). When it happened again we took tools out so we could replace the shear pins underwater. It took us three days of rigging and re-rigging cable, of repairing broken equipment, of nightly arguments between Jim and me, until we were finally able to loosen the rock. After three days of work I was able to film the griphoist doing its job. At last the Wedge Rock lay in the gravel like a great dead tooth. And the huge ledge had not dropped down on the *Nephripod*—or on us.

9. UNDER THE LEDGE

THE DAY AFTER we extracted the Wedge Rock the weather turned nasty. We buried the crowbar and chains in gravel under the ledge and were able to remove the other equipment before the sea came up. By ten we began our final gear-laden climb up the cliff. By this time white-caps covered the ocean clear to the horizon. It was noon when the last of the equipment was carried into camp and three o'clock by the time we had washed the salt off of everything, stowed it in the trailer, and headed home.

Halfway to Monterey, as I rounded Hurricane Point my knuckles whitened on the wheel as gusts of wind threatened to force the VW off the road. I was reminded that we still faced a long siege of winter storms.

Gary had a change of plans. He suddenly ran out of money. Also, the ski season was still in full swing, so off he went to the Sierras, to the promise of a job on the slopes—and the waiting arms of the snow bunnies. He returned to the Cove throughout the remaining winter for limited engagements only. At such times he hinted at fantastic high altitude romances, leaving most of the details of his adventures to our vivid imaginations.

Now that the Wedge Rock was out we were ready to pull the *Nephri-pod* loose. But we continued to break shear pins, so Jim picked up a larger griphoist, one capable of five tons of pull.

Jim had been promising to quit his job. Finally, at a point of pride where a showdown was imminent, he didn't back down. Once he had quit he drove to Clear Lake to finish the jade trailer.

For me it was the start of a new semester, and I re-immersed myself in academia.

The new year began with blue skies and calm seas. Jim telephoned from Clear Lake to say that he had finished the trailer and had had it weighed and safety-checked. Now we were ready to move the *Nephri-pod.*

Jim and I headed south again. We arrived at Jade Cove about noon, our spirits high. As I unloaded the big griphoist from the back of the Bronco I thought, *this tool will do the trick!*

While Jim organized things at camp I dove to see if anyone had taken the crowbar or the chains. They were still where we had left them. I inspected the *Nephripod,* realizing that the huge ledge by the Cave

Rock actually hung down over its uppermost tip. There was less than an inch between them where the two surfaces overlapped. We had concentrated so hard on removing the Wedge Rock that we had somehow forgotten this. But now it was plain that the overhang would keep us from pulling the rock straight out and that if the *Nephripod* were raised at all it would shift tight against the ledge when it was moved. I also saw that one end of the *Nephripod* was under the Cave Rock, so the *Nephripod* would have to be pulled away from the Cave Rock before it could be pulled toward the Gravel Pit. In other words, it would have to be pulled south, parallel to shore, and then toward shore, in a "one-two" operation.

The next day I put chain around the *Nephripod,* manipulating it behind where I couldn't reach by using special tools Jim had fashioned out of steel reinforcing bar. Once the chain was secure I laid cable around several other submerged rocks. I hooked the new griphoist on and started pumping.

As I was working a diver swam up to watch. Since it was Sunday and I was used to weekend spectators, I ignored the diver's presence, hoping he'd go away. He did, and as I watched him dissolve into the cloudy water, threading his way along the cable toward the *Nephripod,* I cursed silently. I didn't like other divers looking at "our rock." I soon forgot him though, and went back to work.

A little later I felt a tap on my shoulder. The other diver had come back. He beckoned me toward the *Nephripod* and I swam after him reluctantly, thinking as I went that I would humor him so that maybe he would go away and leave me to my task. Once at the *Nephripod* he conveyed by sign language that I should bring the rock out toward the Gravel Pit and not in the direction I was pumping. I made a sign of disagreement, showing him where the *Nephripod* was up against the Cave Rock. Then I put one finger up and motioned in the direction I was pulling, then two fingers up and motioned toward the Gravel Pit. He seemed to understand. He looked the rock over again carefully, gave me the universal O.K. sign, and swam away. I went back to work.

Propping my feet up on the surrounding rocks and pushing with my shoulder, I strained with my back and legs against the handle, working it forward, then changing position for the backward stroke.

After a time I swam over to look at the *Nephripod.* To my amazement I had moved it a quarter of an inch! Then we *could* move it! But unfortunately it was now touching the ledge. I studied the two surfaces, suddenly realizing that to get the *Nephripod* by we would have to break off the ledge.

I swam ashore to tell Jim the bad news. I also told him about the underwater spectator. I said that he must be an experienced diver, because we carried on an underwater conversation and he seemed to understand everything I said. Jim motioned seaward and told me that it was Ernie Porter. That explained it.

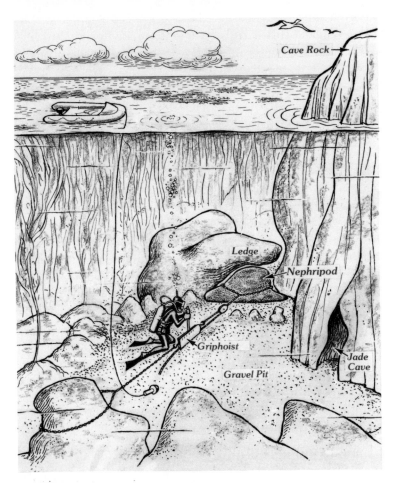

The *Nephripod* is loosened with the griphoist.

Ernie is one of the most remarkable divers I have ever met. He is a commercial abalone diver from Morro Bay, short, wiry, and very strong. He has uncontrollable jade fever, like the rest of us, and on his days off from commercial diving he comes to the Cove. He has a reputa- for making a single tank last a long, long time. I have friends who have

seen Ernie walking in through the surf with his fins in one hand and a
sack of jade and a crowbar over his shoulder. He knows Jade Cove like
the back of his hand, usually finding more and better jade on a given day
than any other diver in the water. He has taken out large rocks—one
which weighed close to 2,000 pounds he took out singlehandedly.

I was out in the water again, moving the cable to get another
purchase on the rock, when Ernie came ashore. Jim later told me that
Ernie said we had taken on a "Herculean task." I felt good about his
remark.

Now that the *Nephripod* would budge no farther our next job was to
chip off the ledge. This was more than we had bargained for, since we
soon discovered that the ledge itself was jade—poor quality, but none-
theless jade. Jade's fibrous structure makes it one of the most durable
of minerals. That is why it can be sculpted and worn by the abrasion and
beating it gets in the sea but is hardly ever chipped or broken.

Our efforts to chop through the jade overhanging ledge were frustrating. Now capable of using three to five tanks a day, I spent a solid week
with a sledge hammer, chisels, and crowbar, working alone, Jim
carrying tanks up and down the cliff. Although my arm grew sore from
swinging the sledge and Jim's back stiff from carrying tanks, our efforts
were of little avail.

One day Gary appeared in camp, and both of us worked into the
second week. Ernie Porter swam out and had at it with some of his
chisels, then on shore gave both of us a basic lesson on how to split
rocks by using special chisels, made of malleable steel, which follow the
fracture lines. These chisels were small and very thin, and Ernie demon-
strated how the soft points could follow the erratic fractures in large
rocks, almost effortlessly popping them open. Later we bought some of
these chisels at a specialty house in San Francisco and returned to
attack the ledge again. But we could only split off a few small pieces—
not enough to bring the *Nephripod* through. There just weren't any
large fractures we could open.

Although Jim was opposed to it, Gary and I decided secretly that if all
else failed we would dynamite the ledge. Sometime when Jim wasn't
around we would do the job early in the morning or late in the evening.
Sure it was illegal, but what the hell....

Gary spread the word to friends at school that we could use a dynamite expert. San Francisco State had been staggered by riots during
the 1969-70 school year, and while President Hayakawa had all but

snuffed out the problem there was still an aftermath of tension on campuses across the nation in early 1971. Most students were playing it cool. Therefore I was completely unprepared when one day as I was walking between classes a voice rang out behind me:

"Hey Wobber, I got a dynamiter for you!"

I couldn't believe it. Images of police with riot clubs charging down the halls looking for suspicious characters were still vivid in my memory. If the wrong people heard the word "dynamiter" we could both take a quick trip to the local hoosegow, probably with a good thump on the skull to boot. I turned around. It was Vic, one of my classmates.

"Sh-h-h-h-h," I whispered, "I'll talk to you later."

When I questioned Vic later he revealed that he did in fact have an ex-demolition man lined up, who had access to all the necessary equipment. I told him I would let him know.

During the spring semester I had arranged my schedule so that I had a heavy load on Tuesday and Thursday and was free Monday, Wednesday, and Friday. This gave me a four-day weekend, or, if I cut one day of classes, a six-day weekend, so that I could devote most of the next four months to The Rock.

Ski season was in full swing and Gary was back with the snow bunnies, so I did most of the underwater work alone, with Jim backing me up topside. As I worked on the ledge the sea's strength seemed to grow within me, sweeping into my body until it seemed to become my very presence. As if by some primitive design the sea held me to its own timetable, one which my own judgement had no effect on. I was alone and whole and totally absorbed in my task. Each night I eased my bruised and aching body into my sleeping bag, not altogether unhappily shifting to feel each stiff joint, each cut, or rubbing each bruise, satisfying myself that this aching hulk would somehow function again the following day.

Jim would say, "You and Gary could work on the ledge together—if Gary were here. But we can't count on that."

And I'd reply, "He'll be along. At least he told me he would."

And Gary would always show up, eventually. When he came he was a celebration—full of life and good spirits. With him there we always had lots of laughs.

Although progress on chipping the ledge was slow, we made small amounts of headway each day. I made a pact with myself to devote a solid month to the ledge, with brief school breaks in between, and only after that month was over to measure my success by how much had been accomplished. Then I would decide whether to keep on chipping for another month.

10. HOMAGE TO THE GODS

I CAN'T SAY what was happening to Jim or Gary, but I was gradually slipping into a more simplified life. The water, the weather, the bruises on my body, the food I ate, and, most important of all, chipping the ledge—these had become my daily existence. They were simple things and required a level of consciousness that I found refreshing. I felt somehow released, enabled to be more in tune with things than ever before. My senses were sharper, as if they had suddenly become totally aware for the first time, as if they had been reborn. I had become a primitive man, free of the bonds that culture and society impose, free as a sea bird. I was free of all worry because I had allowed myself to become obsessed with a completely impractical goal—like the Easter Islanders chipping, transporting, and erecting huge heads of stone to some long-dead god. The ledge had become my "homage to the gods."

Before this, when I had read stories of the hardships of mountain climbers and seen movies of rugged pioneers dropping dead of the plague or starving in the desert, I had always figured that if I were in similar circumstances I would be the first one to die. Therefore, it was a pleasant surprise to learn that despite all my imaginary internal inadequacies I had a really tough system. For a while all my partners were plagued by bad health from time to time, I survived the whole Jade Cove expedition without mishap—except for a few bruises, aching bones, and an occasional hangover.

On a typical day at Jade Cove I would rise early and, if Gary was there, would wake him for our morning excursion, which Gary called our "bunny walk." The bunny walk was an institution. Because of the nature of the unprotected coast, the surf could come up in a matter of hours and make diving impossible, so each morning it was necessary to take a look at the Cove. Gary and I—sometimes the three of us—would head down the path out of camp, where we would see cottontails waiting for us beside the black asphalt road. Usually there were five or six of them, their pink ears erect, their noses twitching. As we came along they would show us their white tails and take turns hopping back into the bushes. After 600 yards or so of walking on the road we turned toward the sea and went over the stile that fronts the meadow above the Cove. We followed a well-worn path down a gentle slope to the brow of the cliff above Jade Cove. All the time we were watching swells come in from the horizon, but unless the ocean was extremely rough we still couldn't tell what the water in the Cove was like until we got to the edge of the cliff. When we got there we would urinate down the face of the cliff, not out of disdain but because it was a ritual.

I would tell of my dreams of the night before, which almost always involved jade, Jim, and Gary in some sort of unearthly struggle, involving complex, unsolvable situations. Sometimes Tarkin was roaming solitarily through these dreams. He seemed far away, as if in a mist, always searching, looking for something he had lost ... as in reality we often caught sight of him looking for jade on a distant cliff or beach. My dreams were not taken seriously.

Then we would look into the water at the base of the rocks below us to see what the visibility was like. When a large ground swell formed we would watch it as it passed silently by the Cave Rock and dissipated on the narrow beach. Leaning on the wood railing at the top of the cliff, we tried to visualize how the surge around the Cave Rock would affect our diving and then decided whether or not we would dive that day.

Most mornings were foggy and damp, and although the tops of the Santa Lucia Mountains, framed by small breaks in the moist and gloomy shroud, were usually tipped with sunlight, the fog along the coast didn't burn off, if at all, until afternoon. It was unusual to have a completely clear morning.

When we got back to the house trailer, our shoes wet and our noses cold, we would have hot coffee, toast, mush, grapefruit, and bacon and eggs. Since Gary didn't drink water, milk, coffee, or any such unhealthy commodities, I would often join him in a small glass of wine.

After breakfast Gary and I would each pick up a tank and our other diving equipment and head down the hill. Jim usually stayed behind to tidy up the camp and then brought more air down to us. The trail to the Cove ends in a jumble of boulders at the bottom of some wooden stairs, and we would thread our way through them. When we reached the beach, which consists entirely of rock, we would throw our gear down and walk to the water's edge to look for a small piece of jade. It meant good luck to find some jade before the dive began.

The day before we had buried our weight belts in the pebbles rather than carry them up the hill, so now we would have to dig them out. We then would begin to suit up, pulling on our damp bathing suits. The pants to our diving suits and the socks I wore under my booties would still be wet and cold from yesterday's dive. Putting on cold gear is the most miserable part of diving.

By the time our first two tanks were drained it would be noon. By the time we got back to the beach we would find that the rockhounds had all but destroyed it by digging huge holes, and as we staggered from the water we would kid them about falling into their trenches. We swapped sea-worn jade pebbles for pieces of botryoidal jade they had found.

Our jade was collected by swimming devious routes out to and back from the *Nephripod*. These side trips cost only a few extra breaths of air, and the little pieces we found we poked in our booties, suit crotches, up our sleeves, and under our hoods. Once ashore, each gem was extracted with the utmost care. Gary hoarded his, claiming he traded them for unspeakable favors from the ladies!

Other divers, combing wider areas, brought in larger and better pieces of jade. Envious of their freedom, we vowed that someday we would use a whole tank of air looking for free pieces. But we never did. During our venture we used more than 200 tanks of air, but not one was used exclusively for such a search.

When on shore, between tanks, we often looked for beach jade and showed tourists who had never found it how to recognize it. When they could not find any themselves we generously gave them small but not very good pieces we had collected.

Sometimes the beach was crowded with rockhounds, digging, picnicking, and shouting to one another. I remember a fat lady from Washington State who was spread out on the beach, digging a hole. Whenever she found a jade pebble she slid it into her mouth, holding it in her cheek. Her cheeks bulged out so much we christened her "Chipmunk Cheeks." At one point she suddenly let out a yelp, "Paydirt, paydirt!" and waved a green gem high above her head.

"Henry, come here, I've struck paydirt!" she called to her husband, as she thrust the green beauty into her mouth.

After winter storms the beach was often littered with rotting kelp, which drew surf-flies in thick clouds. Sometimes loose kelp piled so high that we sat on it to put our fins on before we slid off into the water. It was slimy and dangerous, and when we emerged from the water, to keep ourselves from falling, we had to crawl on all fours over the rubbery mounds until we reached the solid beach.

Then suddenly the next day the kelp and the flies would be gone.

There were also days when the water would be thick with broken kelp floating in large patches—a condition we referred to as "minestrone." When we swam into large patches of minestrone we were suddenly in zero visibility. There were other days when we felt our way blindly about in a rusty, darkened sea, heavy with red tide, and then there were days of just plain poor visiblity. In fact, it was exceptional when we could see more than ten or twenty feet, barely adequate for filming. So I did little filming.

I crawl on all fours out of the water.

One day, however, the visibility was better than usual, so the three of us dove with a movie camera. We had planned to move some large rocks weighing between 400 and 900 pounds out of the Gravel Pit so we could work close in to the *Nephripod*. We put chains on the rocks, clipped half-filled lifting bags to them until the load was just short of buoyant, then bounced the rocks across the sea floor until they were out of the Gravel Pit.

I was filming this procedure when a rock Jim and Gary were working on would not lift, even though it had two bags on it and they were prying it loose with a crowbar. The rock didn't look that difficult to me, and I grew impatient. I handed Gary the camera, grabbed another empty lifting bag, put it on the rock and began filling it. Somehow my regulator got in between the nylon ropes attached to the clips. The rock must have been wedged in, because all at once it came loose and shot toward the surface. The ropes tightened around my regulator and I shot up with the rock. All of a sudden I was on the surface, which surprised the hell out of me. Jim and Gary were convulsed with laughter.

"Ha, ha," indeed! If I hadn't had the intuition to keep the expanding air in my lungs flowing out of my mouth on the quick trip up I could have blown a lung right out through my rib cage and been floating belly-up by the time they stopped laughing. But since that didn't happen I laughed along with them.

Often when we had used all our air for the day we forgot about the *Nephripod* and free-dove in shallow water. Throwing down our tanks and entering the sea without the binding harness and tanks on our backs allowed us a dimension of freedom it is hard to describe. We liked diving in shallow water under the breakers, an excellent way to pick up small pieces of jade. We learned the wave rhythms, to anticipate the arrival of the next wave (which can knock a diver for a loop in shallow water), and we learned to cling to the short, swaying algae before each surge hit. The red, brown, and green algae moved with the surge, and fish darted in under it and then out into the open again in a perpetual ballet. I don't know of any other type of diving where I feel closer or more in tune with the sea, where I feel as though I belong to it, flowing back and forth with its rhythms much as the fish do.

I remember diving for a small green stone in a deep hole, then, treasure in hand, looking upward to find my way through a sky of tangled kelp. Above me a large school of small metallic surf perch slanted like distant windows in a city's sunset, reflecting light, moving as one as though fixed in their relationship to one another. As I rose through them they scattered before me like broken pieces of the sun, and suddenly were gone.

We spent hours diving this way, and many times the sun was on the horizon when we swam back to the beach. Then we would make the last weary climb of the day up the hill, knowing that our agony would soon end, our last load lifted, our last step taken, the day's job finished.

At the top of the cliff we sometimes threw ourselves down to rest, or leaned against the wooden railing to gaze back at the sea. Below us, the serpentine ocean cliffs, ragged, storm-torn. Often in the darkness of the green beach-rocks there would still be a few eager rockhounds harvesting their strange crop on the beach below. I remember once a sleek cormorant flying close above the surface of the water, making an arc out to sea, then turning up the coast to lose itself against the black shapes of kelp and water-ripple. Then a thin line of gold rimmed the horizon, enclosing the sea to the west, and the moving water below us turned to pink, like the scales of a salmon.

When we reached the campground the lights of the house trailer would be on and Jim would open the door to present me with a beer and Gary with a glass of wine. We would conscientiously rinse out our suits and hose off our itching bodies with ice-cold water. Then we would towel off, step into the damp, warm house trailer, and put on dry clothes.

Cheese was cut into small squares and served with crackers and wine. We sat around the table, around a candleholder we had fashioned out of a fist-sized piece of jade by melting wax and sticking a candle on it. We laughed, told stories, and feasted in the candle-glow, the trailer windows wet with moisture. We displayed our recent jade acquisitions, Jim's taken from a drawer, Gary's from a couple of old socks, and mine from a stainless steel pan. Then the whistle would blow on the pressure cooker and the serious eating began.

Gary and I had a few minor complaints about Jim's cooking as the months wore on—largely due to pressure-cooked meals where potatoes tasted like carrots, which tasted like onions, which tasted like meat. But it was quantitative rather than qualitative eating. Occasionally Gary cooked and we had gourmet Italian cuisine. I am only good at opening cans, so I washed the dishes. Jim liked a certain German wine and would occasionally serve us a bottle, but it often gave Gary and me hangovers the next day (maybe because we overimbibed). Sometimes Gary would show up with some fancy, cheap Japanese wine, or some King George scotch. On such occasions the two of us would get deliciously drunk and yet would still be alive enough to dive the next day.

11. PORTAPOWER

EARLY IN February Jim came up with a new gadget. He purchased a "Portapower," a 20-pound hydraulic device. This was a $145 toy, a cylindrical tool about 14 inches long with a handle on it. Pressure, pumped into the cylinder by moving the handle back and forth, elongates the cylinder and transfers as much as 10,000 pounds of force to a small, chisel-shaped head, giving a tremendous mechanical advantage. Jim guaranteed that it would work on the ledge.

As soon as the weather looked good Gary and I assaulted the ledge with this new weapon. We put it in various positions, chisel head against the ledge and butt end against the Cave Rock, and pumped it up. Nothing happened. We decided to leave it overnight with as much pressure in it as we could pump, reasoning that steady pressure over an extended time might crack the ledge.

From the cliff the next morning the water in Jade Cove looked rough. Not only had there been an earthquake the day before in Los Angeles (the February 9 tremor in the San Fernando Valley that destroyed a section of the San Diego Freeway) but there had also been an eclipse of the moon. I don't know what the earthquake or the eclipse had to do with the ocean, but they must have had some effect. That morning we were unaware of both events. All we knew was that seven or eight large sets of waves would come rolling through, followed by a period of relative calm. The wave pattern kept repeating itself, and by the time Gary and I got to the *Nephripod* it had not changed.

The Portapower was still tight against the ledge, but it had done no good. We left it where it was and went back to chiseling the ledge, one of us using a heavy sledge hammer and a chisel while the other wedged himself in among boulders, holding on to the working man's ankles to keep him in place.

When the next large sets of waves rolled by overhead we abandoned our work and clung to the Portapower. If we let go the powerful surge would hurl us into the Gravel Pit and then toss us back again. We had little control against such power and were easily flung into large rocks. Sand and gravel now pelted us like hail, and rocks weighing up to five pounds occasionally tumbled by. Hanging on, we counted each wave as it swept overhead. When seven or eight surges passed the water calmed, and we could work again.

After half an hour of alternately clinging to the Portapower or chipping away at the ledge a much stronger series of waves began. We clung to the Portapower and counted "seven, eight, nine" but the waves kept coming. The surges grew progressively stronger; we could feel the mounting cold strength of each one against our legs. We hung on to the Portapower desperately. Our feet were pulled loose from their wedged-in positions and our legs were flung out horizontally, fluttering like flags in a gale. Then the returning backwash crumpled us up against the rocks.

We quickly learned not to relax our legs. As the surges continued and kept on building we studied each other quizzically, shrugging our shoulders, each one wondering when it would end and what we should do.

Then it began to grow dark, as if a shade had been drawn. In the dim light the water between us, suddenly filled with swirling bubbles and sand, became a sucking torrent of inconceivable fury.

Although he was only a foot away, I could scarcely make out Gary's features. Finally, I figured we had better get out and get out fast. Between the next incoming surge and the backwash from the former one I signaled to Gary, and we took off for the surface, swimming out and away from the Cave Rock for fear that we might be dashed against it.

We emerged into a terrible, tilted, confused world. Walls of water were smashing against the cliffs in unleashed fury, falling, tearing, beating against them. Patchy meadows of kelp had come to life, disappearing beneath the water under the crest of a wave, and rising out of deep troughs like schools of glistening serpents.

Our float had torn loose and was gone. Gary spotted it to seaward and shouted that he would go after it. I shouted back that I would dive down, free the Portapower, and meet him on the seaward side of the Cave Rock.

I dove back into the darkened cauldron and after a long struggle freed the Portapower. Clutching it under one arm, I held my body head-downward while blowing air into my life vest for buoyancy, all the while being swept twenty to thirty feet in one direction, then back again. I tried to fend myself away from the rocks with my free hand while being hurled past them, but I was not altogether successful. When I surfaced again, the sea looked like the inside of a giant washing machine.

I saw that Gary had caught up with the float, but he was still far seaward. I kicked toward him, but under the weight of the Portapower my life vest was not holding me on the surface. I didn't know it, but a two-inch gash had been torn in the vest, making it useless. Occasionally I gulped water and soon began to cough. When at last Gary and I met it was a great relief to roll the Portapower onto the float and then cling to it.

Gary had been fighting a southerly current; the waves, piling water into the Cove from the north, were draining out to the south. We were being sucked out to sea. The waves were now so huge they were breaking over the Cave Rock. We felt very small. To get to the beach at all we would have to pump like hell parallel to shore, working the float north.

Suddenly we saw a huge swell building up beyond us. We weren't going to make it over the top of it; the swell would break before it got to us, and there was nothing we could do. We swam as hard as we could toward the swell, hauling the float between us. The huge wave formed and broke and a wall of white water advanced. We pushed the float as far north as we dared, then turned it quickly, directly into the wave front. The wall of water crashed down on us head-on. The float was ripped from our hands and flipped skywards. I closed my eyes as I felt a sudden thump on the side of my head, then blackness. I had been hit by the Portapower!

I couldn't have been out for more than a second. When I opened my eyes I was enveloped in a maelstrom of swirling bubbles. I shook off the pain and clawed toward where I imagined the surface was. Above, the sea was surprisingly quiet, a jumble of confused foam.

I was riding seaward on the backwash of the wave. Then another wave struck me. I fought for the bottom until I could fight no more.... Then there was foam and sunlight again—but Gary and the float were nowhere in sight. I was alone, my face mask askew, water stinging my eyes. My hand, no, my head was dripping with blood.

It was a long swim in. Gary had overtaken the float, caught a ride on a few good waves and had made it to the beach. After what seemed to be an eternity I was finally tossed up on the shore by a breaker and managed to crawl up the steep, pebbly beach to safety.

The sea was now tremendous, tearing at the very foundations of the coast, wave upon wave pounding against the beach, shaking the rocks beneath. Fingers of white foam clutched at the highest rocks, and the water returning to the sea rattled the beach pebbles like old bones. The slant of the beach grew steeper as we watched. We were amazed at how quickly the water contoured the beach: the backwash of a single wave could change an area of small pebbles to a trough of fist-sized stones. It was hard to believe that kind of sea could have come up so suddenly. We had been lucky to get out alive.

We lay there looking at the water for a long time.

The sea stayed rough for three weeks.

Winter surf at the Cove.

12. SONNY

BY THE TIME I got back to the Cove again my first series of school examinations was over, and I was free of scholarly worries for over a month. Jim was coming down to the Cove later and Gary was up in the snow, so I was alone.

Since our efforts to break off the ledge had failed, I decided to try a desperate approach—to dig under the *Nephripod* as far as I could reach with a shovel and a garden hoe, in hope of lowering it enough to clear the ledge either while we worked on it or when we pulled it with the griphoist. I discovered a flat rock under the outer edge of the *Nephripod* and put a house jack on top of it and tightened it up against the jade. Now I could work underneath without fear that the *Nephripod* would come down on top of me. I tried to dig with the shovel, but each little bit of sand or gravel I picked up was washed away by the surge before it could be moved out of the hole. The garden hoe, however, was a wonderful tool. Not only could fairly good-sized rocks be loosened and dragged out from hard-to-reach places, but gravel and sand could be pulled away with one long stroke.

I soon ran into a hard grey clay which had rocks imbedded in it. Silt from the disturbed clay enveloped me in dense clouds of fine sediment, so I learned to work by feel. After working blindly in this suspended material and not knowing whether I was really making any progress I had to swim away from the area periodically to let the sediment settle.

One day I was doing some free diving in shallow water along the north side of the Cove when I came across a large flat rock of about 1200 pounds tied with heavy line. I looked it over. The rock was jade, but not of a very good quality. I knew that Ernie wouldn't tie up a dog like that, and I wasn't aware that any of the other divers working the Cove could handle such a rock.

Back on shore I met a diver in his early twenties whose crew-cut made him appear as though he had just been released from the Service (which wasn't far from wrong). His name was Sonny Phillips. He looked sunny too, his round, sunburned face resembling a brightly polished apple with a wide smile sliced in it. His ears rose two inches every time he laughed.

He seemed to know jade. He asked me if I had seen the rock he had tied up and what I thought of it. Although I had looked it over carefully, I told him I hadn't really looked at it closely but I wasn't too impressed with what I'd seen. He didn't think much of it either and said he was thinking of giving it up.

We talked for a while. Then he asked if I knew of a small rock wedged between the Cave Rock and another large rock, on the seaward side. I had been aware of it but hadn't paid much attention to it because of its difficult location and because the jade on one side didn't look very good. He asked me if I would take another look.

I went back into the water and saw that the bottom side of the rock was good. So for the next couple of days we both worked on separate rocks about twenty feet from each other. Sonny borrowed the crowbar. I helped him and he helped me. I could sometimes hear him pounding on rock as I was hoeing under the *Nephripod*. "Heigh-ho, heigh-ho..." kept running through my mind. We were like two of the most industrious of Snow White's seven dwarfs.

Jim arrived at the Cove and a day later Gary showed up, and I talked to them about Sonny. He lived with his sister at Cambria, about 50 miles to the south, and was trying to make a living diving for jade. It was an old story—there have been lots of divers who were going to make it diving for jade, but they never make it. However, Sonny lived nearby and might be a valuable addition to our team. I liked him. He was open and honest. He had a solid, strong body, muscular yet lithe, and he handled himself efficiently underwater. Since he was planning to spend a lot of time at the Cove he could keep an eye on our equipment when we weren't there. He was broke, and I suggested that we could pay him to work for us, exchange labor, or take him in on a partnership basis.

Gary now had a good job offer, and while he would be able to get off work when we really needed him, he was not free to put in the days of monotonous work that we now felt were necessary, so he offered to reduce his share in the rock to let Sonny in. Jim agreed to let Sonny in too, so we advanced him some cash to take care of his immediate needs. I think Sonny was surprised at this and appreciated our trust. Our project gained a good man, and I gained the help of another diver.

13. THE GREEN PICKLE

NOW WE were four. The age mix was unusual—Jim in his mid-fifties, me in my mid-forties, Gary twenty-seven, and Sonny going on twenty-one. But the group was held together by the bond of a singular purpose, and it worked well.

At first Sonny was wary of us. It occurred to us that he might have been taken advantage of by someone once and was not about to let it happen again. But gradually, after he finally broke his rock loose and we helped him drag it up the hill, he began to accept us.

A month earlier, while resetting a cable to loosen the *Nephripod,* I had found a piece of jade about four and a half feet long, shaped like a huge green pickle. It was alongside the Gravel Pit where hundreds of divers search and where we had been diving for months. Although jade is generally easy to spot, this rock was almost completely covered with a pink plant encrustation called coralline algae. I loosened this "Green Pickle" with a crowbar, marked the spot, then threw some rocks over it to hide it and continued working on the cable.

Jim and I estimated that the Green Pickle weighed about 600 pounds. It was too large to take up the cliff, so we decided to raise it, pull it out to sea through the heavy shore kelp, and tow it down the coast to bring it in at Willow Creek. Since we had planned to use the same route to remove the *Nephripod,* and since neither of us had brought out any rocks in this way for years, we thought it would be a good practice run for us and a good way for Sonny to gain experience with our methods.

We decided that Sonny was to fill the bags with air and raise the rock. Then while Jim and I were towing it he would drive down to Willow Creek and help us beach it.

In preparation for hauling the *Nephripod* we had purchased a new "Seagull," a rugged and reliable English-made outboard motor with a power propeller especially designed to move bulky loads at slow speeds. We felt confidence in its reliability and power. Although Jim had tested the Seagull at Clear Lake, pulling the Green Pickle to Willow Creek was its maiden salt-water run.

We wrapped the Green Pickle in a net and hooked on six lifting bags. Sonny raised the rock without incident. It was a good lift, with all six bags protruding at least five inches above the water line and the bottom of the Green Pickle about four feet beneath the water's surface. While

Sonny swam back to shore I hooked on to it from the Speedyak with the tow rope.

Jim was having trouble getting the new motor started, so I used the oars to keep us moving slowly seaward. Jim re-read the Seagull instruction booklet as I rowed the Speedyak, towing the Green Pickle on a zig-zag course through the kelp. Then he pulled the starter rope a couple of times until the motor finally kicked over. It putted and spluttered for about ten minutes, taking us away from the Cove, before it died. I began to row again.

The ground swells were showing some strength. We felt their smooth rolling power moving swiftly and silently beneath us, first lifting us so we could see the whole shoreline to the east, then dropping us gently down again into deep troughs where we were alone with the sea and the thick tangled kelp beds that threatened to catch on to the load we were towing. After they passed us the backs of the ground swells metamorphosed into raging breakers that pounded the shoreward rocks with unleashed fury and left trails of foamy white bubbles in their wake. Water vapor blew off the combs of the breakers and drifted upward in misty clouds toward the cliffs. Beyond the white water the surf ran up small gravel-lined beaches and beat against the towering coastal cliffs.

I pulled hard on the oars. They felt like toys in my hands. The shafts were about as thick as a broomstick and they had no handgrips. The blades were made of thin plywood which bent at every stroke, threatening to split. Also, if I pulled too hard the plastic oarlocks twisted out of the mooring holes.

Above us I could hear the wind, at a higher pitch than the pounding of the surf. Its agonizing shriek was ominous, and we looked up to see an occasional wisp of cloud scudding toward the shore. It was this ghost-like wind, neither felt nor seen, that must have been driving the mammoth swells in from the sea.

Both Jade Cove and Willow Creek seemed very far away now. If something happened the shore would be no refuge, even if we could make it through the surf to one of the beaches. The cliffs were so high and sheer that if we were to be stranded we would have to rely on helicopter rescue to get out safely. On the tops of the precipitous cliffs toy cars edged along the highway, weaving in and out of sight—so near and yet so far.

Jim bent over the motor, talking to it, gently swearing at it. My hands were sore; the oars were pulling on skin that had been softened by months of diving. The wind was rising, and we were making little progress. We were threading our way at a snail's pace through scattered beds of kelp. The afternoon was darkening into evening. The sea seemed poised and about to explode.

Suddenly it all seemed futile. I said, "You know, Jim, we're nothing but old fools out in the middle of the ocean, towing a huge green pickle."

We laughed at our own sense of futility, and then we looked at the ocean and cursed. Finally, at long last the Seagull started again. I leaned back to relax, and then it died and I rowed some more. The oars had loosened the skin on my palms, twisting it into wide white blisters, and I could feel a pain mounting in my back. I wondered whether we had entangled Sonny and Gary, our wives, and a lot of other people in a nightmarish dream that was too big for two old fools to handle. I also wondered whether we would ever be able to pull the *Nephripod* to Willow Creek.

The Seagull motor and I had shared equally in time, if not distance, in powering the Green Pickle. When we were just north of Willow Creek the sun began to set. The wind miraculously, had died down.

Finally the Seagull started again, and we brought the rock in swiftly, close to the surf line. Jim threw a line overboard and I went over the side. Since the surf was still running high, Jim took the Speedyak to the sheltered side of the north point, where the water was relatively calm, and beached her.

I grabbed the line and swam for shore, tugging on the Green Pickle. Sonny had already arrived. He swam out and joined me, and we pulled the rock into the surf. It might seem dangerous to bring a heavy rock buoyed by lifting bags through a storm surf, but we had learned that if you attach a long line to the rock and don't try to ride it in, it is quite safe—actually the easiest part of the whole operation. The rock, because of its weight, comes in slowly, pushed shoreward but bypassed by the swiftly moving waves. The weight of the rock keeps the lifting bags solidly down, even when the breakers crash down on top of it. If the tow rope is long enough the rock can more or less be guided in.

For a while there was bedlam when the Green Pickle was washed up onto the beach. We tried to hold it in the surf, one diver braced against it to keep it in position while the other removed the bags. The ropes on the bags were tangled and the bags, now filled with water and sand, were heavy and moved the rock as the waves caught them. All the while the waves hit us from one direction and the backwash from another, knocking us flat out in a tangle of bags, ropes, and net. Because of its cigar-like shape the Green Pickle rolled over easily, sometimes on our hands and feet.

Once the bags were removed it was easy to move but it was still dangerous because an occasional backwash from a high wave would turn it around or roll it on us. However, we finally maneuvered it far up on the beach and tied it to the cliff for the night.

Jim and I were down on the beach early the next day. The tide was out and our prize was high and dry.

Moving a 400-pound piece of jade through the boulders on a car hood.

We had brought an old car hood to use upside-down as a sled and were in the process of tying the jade to it when we saw a tall, lanky man of about sixty coming toward us along the beach. He had deepset eyes that looked out from under bushy grey eyebrows and he wore a wide-brimmed cowboy hat and boots. He introduced himself as Hank. He was a salty, extremely friendly old guy who could talk the legs off a centipede. He looked our jade over and decided he liked it.

We were about to rig the griphoist to the car hood when Hank volunteered his services and those of his two teenage sons, who were nearby. We found a strong tree branch about fourteen feet long and used it as a yoke by throwing a loop of chain around it, which we then attached to the hood. The five of us lined up behind the tree branch and dragged the

Jim on the griphoist, Jade Cove.

Green Pickle on the car hood across the beach. We must have created a picturesque scene, our breaths vaporizing in the crisp morning air as, like a team of dray horses, we pulled the huge rock down the beach through the sea mist.

When we got to the rocky area we used the griphoist for a while. But we were not satisfied with our forward progress, so we hooked a cable to the Bronco and pulled the rock by driving the Bronco forward on the road across the creek. But the Green Pickle hood caught on some rocks, then flipped wildly ahead, catapulting the jade off and nearly wiping out one of Hank's sons.

We abandoned towing with the Bronco and reverted to the griphoist again. This way we could move the rock along slowly enough so that any binding of the hood could be relieved and it could be manipulated easily through the rocks by lifting the forward edges with crowbars.

The sun was out now, and I had my shirt off. I rolled up my pants legs and let the creek water flow into my boots as I adjusted the griphoist cables in the middle of Willow Creek. As I pumped the griphoist the jade inched steadily toward the Bronco. The others moved rocks out of the way and worked with crowbars. There was much shouting. It was refreshing to splash around in the cool water in the heat of the morning sun. I forgot my blistered hands of the previous day, my strength suddenly renewed in a body that had grown hard with months of strenuous work.

We finally got the rock up to the Bronco. We towed it behind the Bronco on a short cable, around the first bend in the road, and then cut it loose from the car hood. We backed the Bronco down the bank so that the bed of the vehicle was slightly below the upper road. Then we made a bridge of boards, eased the Green Pickle down into the bed of the Bronco, and suddenly the job was done.

Later we hauled the Green Pickle to Jim's cabin in Lake County, where it sits today.

14. GOLD MINES AND ANCIENT RIVERS

HANK invited us to his campfire for coffee. It was good to sit around a campfire in the sunshine listening to him talk. He told us that he had mined this area for gold years ago. He had a mine up on the hill above us and used to come down to the creek to sluice out the gravel.

"There was a bunch of people come down to the creek, you know, like rockhounds come down, an' I was mining there. An' I was panning gold. And they said 'You're missing the boat, man, you're mining for gold, an' you've got jade down here which is worth more'n that gold.' "

" 'Jade? What're you talking about?' I'd never seen jade before."

Hank motioned toward the beach where we had just been. "So they took me down the beach there, you know, where the rock sticks out in the water an' the water comes up around it. They said, 'You sit up here an' you watch down there. See that bright one down there?' An' this guy jumps off, you know, an' he grabs it an' he runs like the devil to get out of the way of the wave. Brought it up an' showed it to me, an' I says, 'Yeah, yeah, I see that!' 'Well,' he says, 'that comes pink, it looks white. An' it's green, an' it's blue.' So he says, 'You watch. Anything that's greasy when you pick it up—that's it.' I says, 'O.K. ....' "

Jim said, "Wait a minute, he was wrong about that. Serpentine's greasy, but it's not jade. It's a matter of shape and hardness and translucence."

"Yeah," Hank continued, not to be stopped by minor technicalities, "But anyway, I know now. So anyway, why here come a real bad storm. I mean, it was terrible. You could hear it. Me an' my partner had a lean-to way up the creek, an' we thought the water was going to hit us way up there. But it never did."

"So next morning I went down an' the water had calmed some, y'know, so I run down there, on this rock. I was sitting up there 'on the thing. Well every seventh wave is a big one, y'know, so I wait 'til a big one come, when it would go out again. I'd say, 'Well, I can jump if anything's there.' Well, nothing's there. An' it gets down to about four waves. On the fifth wave, why here's a nice piece, big as my fist. I jump off an' I grabbed that thing, an' the wave hit me. Drove me up over the rocks, an' then down over them. I was cut, bruised, y'know, all over. But I held onto it, I got it out."

"That's the way a lot of the old-timers do," Jim added. "They still like to get jade out that way. They watch the jade slide in with the waves. It seems to retain the water longer than the other rocks; it sparkles and it shines and flashes, and you can tell that it's jade."

Hank added that while he was getting his piece of jade his daughter was up on the bank, away from the surf. "I says, 'I don't mind getting hurt, but I don't want you hurt.' While I'm digging around, getting tore to pieces by them rocks an' everything, she found a beautiful piece of jade. An' I couldn't talk her out of it. I couldn't buy it from her, or nothing. She's still got it. She had two hearts made out of it."

Hank said that if we weren't doing anything the next day he would show us his old mine claim. In the meantime he wanted us to look at a jade rock he had spotted toward the north end of the beach and to tell him if we thought it was good jade.

That afternoon we walked up the beach, searching for jade pebbles along the way. But when we got to the end of the beach we couldn't find Hank's rock.

The next day we drove up a road behind Willow Creek campground to see Hank's mine claim. On a plateau about 100 feet above the highway we got out of the car and walked across a flat shelf of land. Just below the plateau on the hillside facing Willow Creek Hank pointed to the brush-filled scar of his abandoned mine shaft. Far below we could see the highway bridge straddling Willow Creek ravine.

Hank hadn't been the first man to look for gold in this country. More than 100 years ago many gold mines were worked throughout the coast ranges. In the late 1800's at the top of Willow Creek Pass, there had been a gold-mining town, Manchester, with a population of 350. Nothing remains of it now. Indians and Chinese coolies were used to work the extensive mines. I could imagine how the Chinese laborers, after a day's work, might have slipped down to the shore to search the beaches for jade.

Hank told us how about twenty years before he had met a man 75 or 80 years old who was digging for gold on the south side of that same plateau.

"The old man told me all about some Chinese convicts that were working an illegal gold mine. He said it was on the side hill somewheres. He'd been in it when he was a kid, but someone filled it in an' he didn't know where it was.

"I went over to the side cliff where the old man pointed an' saw the hill heavy with scrub brush all tangled and twisted together; impossible to tell where anything was. So I got out my gold dowser I invented, an' it works too, like a water-witch stick, y'know, a forked branch, an' you hold the two ends in each hand an' the free end dips down an' tells where the water's at. But mine's made of metal; it's got a twisted piece of metal around the free end. But anyway, it works. So I took the two ends an' held it out in front an' wandered all up and down that hill. I beat through that brush for about three hours before the free end of that dowser dipped down, an' it dipped down right at the site of that mine. I cleared the brush away and sure enough there was the old shaft going clear into the mountain. So I filed a claim and worked it 'til the Forestry, or someone, burned up my lean-to an' caved in the shaft. They wanted me out of there so they could build a campsite on this land. But they never.

"I had a big ton-and-a-half truck an' took gravel from that mine down to Willow Creek an' panned it. If I sluiced it, it would mess the water up, and they didn't want it messed up because of the steelheads coming up the creek.

"Looked like the Chinese had went in twenty feet an' the bedrock come kinda to a V on the bottom. All this flat rock an' sand an' gravel on the bottom. In fact, when you'd pull it like this," he cupped his hand and drew it through the air, "you could see it: little garnets an' rubies; also, once in a while, you'd see flecks of gold. Free gold in the river. We found pieces as big as my fingernail in there. We were doing real good an' we got into gravel that was the same size as dollars, an' flat, from an old river bed, an' we run into large garnets, an' rubies.

"I found a book in there that was written in Chinese. When we opened the wood on the side of the shaft we took the book out and opened it, an' it just disintegrated. Couldn't do nothing with it. We took a knife and went through it, it was so hard, an' we opened it up like this, an' we got four or five places where there was pictures of Chinese an' Chinese writing, an' about four hours later when we started down with a load of gravel, the paper had fell apart. Just blew away.

"These Chinese that worked the mine were convict labor, the road crew for the Coast Highway in the early 1900's. The compound they lived in was up to the plateau. The Chinese went in there an' they got the gravel out an' then they went down to the creek to pan it for gold. Y'know, it's quite a ways down to the creek. I got permission to blast in there. There was a great enormous rock right at the front of this cave, an' we blowed that off, and it blowed the false bedrock out an' there's an old channel underneath, but we don't know what's in it. There's another river bed underneath of the one we're on, an' I stll think the Chinese went under that rock. We probably worked the upper one only.

"But the Chinese kept the mine secret from the other convicts, kept it covered over all the time—got out around $4,000. Then the others found out about it, but not where the mine was. I don't know how the Chinese kept it secret, but they did. They tried to find out where it was—threatened to cut off the Chinese' pigtails an' everything else.

Cutting those queues off, their souls can't go to heaven. But these guys didn't tell nothing. So they just whacked their hair off. I don't know what they did after that. If they killed them or what happened."

Jim said, "I recall a news story about eight years ago. Some old skeletons were found in a cave on the side hill here, couldn't be but a quarter mile from your mine. We went up there after that, but we didn't have a light, so we only went in so far. There was a narrow passageway between two big rocks, then it dropped straight into nothing. We threw rocks down and heard them bounce for a long time, then thud on the bottom."

Hank remembered the cave, "It was on the side hill, up above. I went up to it, but I never found nothin'."

Jim said, "The papers said they found about ten bodies, most of them Indians, and one or two white men...."

"Or most of them Chinese," Hank added. "They both have high cheek bones. How could they tell?"

"Think they were the convicts?"

"I always thought it was, because there's no Indian artifacts in the area. I did a lot of mining there an' never found any artifacts."

Subsequently, we were to hear other stories about the cave. One of the local mountain people told me nine Indians and one Spaniard were found and that a friend of his had found some gold doubloons in there. He said the cave consisted of seven chambers, each deeper than the last. The bodies were in the deepest chamber.

One of the descendants of the pioneers in the area, John Harlen, told us that the cave had been sealed. He didn't know whether the skeletons were of Indians or a construction crew. Ralph Gould, the area Ranger at the time the skeletons were discovered, said the cave consists of three levels or chambers 100 feet below the level of the entrance. Shortly after the bones were found he posted the cave and blocked the entrance to keep people out, since someone could easily get killed fooling around in there. Ralph said that after the skeleton story reached some of the old-timers in the area they figured out whose bodies they were. One remembered his great-grandfather recalling a gold heist from the town of Manchester, and at the same time nine Indian laborers and one white man disappeared. No one knew what had happened to them or to the gold until the news story about the skeletons was printed and the old-timers put two and two together.

However, if this story is true the question still remains: how, by whom, and why were these men killed? And what became of the gold they stole? Is it still sealed off inside the cave?

Hank pointed out a horizontal line of rock across the canyon which was at approximately the same elevation as the ground we stood on.

"See that line? These mountains connected when the earth was new."

He kicked a rock out of the soil and handed it to Jim. "This here's river-bottom rock. This was the mouth of an enormous large river that stretched from here clear over to that mountain." His gnarled hand swung in an arc, which also cut through a vast dimension of time.

Through his eyes I saw a geologic age when the earth shifted rapidly, so that the large valley before me was suddenly filled with land. A river had opened here, perhaps a torrent from some faraway, long-forgotten mountain range. I tried to imagine how such a torrent might have entered the sea. In all likelihood, at one time Willow Creek fed into the ocean far to the west of the present shoreline, and its waters, at a time when rainfall was heavier, brought down the gold that Hank, and before him the Chinese coolies, had mined. I visualized the steady uplifting of the Coast range and a simultaneous wearing and cutting of the river slicing knifelike down through the valley of Willow Creek, perhaps even as its source waters were being changed by the drop in rainfall and the sagging, uplifting, slipping, and folding of the interior mountain ranges and valleys. As the source mountains of this once large river evolved so did the river itself; gradually its flow dwindled from a large and once-important system to its present status as a creek.

"This is an ancient river bed," Hank was saying, "river-bottom land. Before the rangers run me off, I had reached the gold. It's still here, twenty feet below us. But now I'm too old...."

Hank looked down at the dusty red soil, his bushy eyebrows furled, as though he could see down through the ground to the gold nuggets that lay beneath his feet.

15. CLEARING A PATH

DURING the rest of the winter and into spring we worked alternately chipping on the ledge and hoeing under "the rock." Our obsession with the project, if anything, had grown stronger. But in addition to school I had some real estate I was neglecting, so I went back to San Francisco whenever I could to try to keep things patched together.

My wife seemed to understand—although I was not convinced that beneath her calm acceptance she wasn't a little concerned. One day she said, "You know, you're not getting a rock, you're creating a work of art!" That's it! A work of art! And the best part was that she appeared to support it.

As for my schoolwork, I let it slide, already having decided that the rock was more important.

I had a diving-biology project going on in Monterey, a study of the natural history of a subtidal sea star, which required large amounts of underwater observational time. On the first of May I threw my diving gear into my VW bus and headed south to work on my Monterey project. Just before Monterey the highway skirts the bay, so that one can judge to a certain extent what the water will be like for diving. That particular day the water was as calm as a mill pond.

At the turnoff for Monterey I felt as if I couldn't control my VW. It seemed to turn south of its own accord, heading toward Jade Cove. So I scrapped my biology project for the time being and went where my VW was taking me.

I met Sonny at the Cove and we dove to inspect the *Nephripod*. We had dug up to three feet deep beneath the whole exposed side. We removed the house jack and rigged the griphoist to see if we could pull the *Nephripod* from under the ledge. When we applied pressure, though, we broke a hook. When we rigged up again the chain slipped off. It turned out to be a frustrating day. I decided I should never have gone to the Cove.

The next morning Sonny went home and Jim and Gary arrived. The water had grown extremely rough, so we went to Willow Creek to smooth out a "roadway" on the south beach in preparation for beaching our rock.

We were rolling some large boulders out of the way when under one of them we found three *Trimusculus reticulata,* a small limpet-like sea snail which has lungs and is related to the common garden snail.

Because my invertebrate professor, Dr. Beeman, had made such a big deal out of these mollusks when his invertebrate class found them at low tide in a sea cave off Tomales Head, I thought they were rare and only found in caves. I decided they should be preserved at all costs. I searched my car for some preservative, but couldn't find any. Then Gary came to the rescue with some King George scotch he had been saving. I thought of Dr. Beeman looking the specimens over while trying to identify the strange smell emanating from the jar.

Finally we had cleared a path on the beach. It looked as if we would be able to move the *Nephripod* over it without much trouble.

16. INDIAN JADE

THE TIDE came in and we moved higher. We were rolling over a large boulder when Jim gleefully jumped into the vacated hole to grab a piece of "Indian jade."

Since the Indians of Willow Creek had no pottery in which to cook their food, they cooked it in asphaltum-lined baskets into which they put heated rocks to warm their acorn mush or other food. Some of the rocks they used were jade. We tried their technique, using an old pot, and discovered that heated jade will boil a pot full of water instantly. Many such heating stones have been found in Indian shell mounds in the area. The jade is easily identified, since it is "burned" on the outside from the Indian fires, which turns it a dull yellow-black.

That night in the house trailer we had a candlelight dinner, graced with a new table decoration—Jim's piece of Indian jade. After dinner Gary and I worked at polishing off what was left of the King George scotch, while Jim drank coffee. Naturally, our conversation turned to Indians. I had developed an interest in the local Indians years back when Ralph Gould, the U.S. Forest Ranger in charge of the campground, had told me about a skeleton that was found at Kirk Creek, just a few miles up the road.

It seems that the rangers had been putting in a holding tank for water when the bulldozer made a cut in the bank that exposed the feet of an Indian skeleton. They stopped working and Ralph went to get some archeologists from the University of California who were digging at Willow Creek.

As Ralph told me, "Two of them went in there with camel-hair brushes, and they took their time. Worked for days. I ain't a-kiddin' you at all; it was like they had a million dollars there in their hands and they just played with it. That's what they were doing. When they got through they had a perfect Indian skeleton, and he had an arrowhead in his skull."

When Ralph found out I was interested in Indians he invited me to his house. He had a collection of arrowheads, rock mortars, and other things, and he told me he had dug up another Indian skeleton behind his house which had seven arrowheads in its rib cage.

Later I went to the University of California Anthropology Library and read a student's doctoral thesis on the Willow Creek Indians. It seems that there were two rival tribes that lived in the interior valley, both of which came over the Willow Creek pass because it was the lowest pass across the Santa Lucias. The tribes collected abalone shells, mussels, and olive shells, which they used for money and trading and made into fishhooks and earrings and which they then traded with tribes farther inland for things they didn't have, like obsidian. The two rival tribes fought with each other over the resources on the coast. The student who wrote the thesis had dug up twelve skeletons at Willow Creek, most of them scalped. The Willow Creek area had been a battleground, a sort of no-man's land for the two tribes.

I told Jim and Gary that the student's thesis said the Indians only used jade as hammers to pound abalone meat or acorns and for heating food.

Gary said, "And they must have used jade to trade with."

"Sure, they used it to gain favors from the cute Indian broads inland. No, he found no indication that they ever used it as pocket pieces or ornaments. The jade was too hard. They couldn't drill or shape it."

"I don't know, I think they did use jade to trade with," Jim said. "Look at the pieces of unburned jade in the shell mounds." He got out a small jar of goodies he had collected that afternoon and dumped the contents on the table. There were pieces of abalone, mussel shells, limpet shells, and one olivella shell with the tip knocked off. The Indians strung the olivella shells as beads and used them for money. There were several small pieces of unburnt jade. One was smooth and especially nice—a perfect touchstone.

I hadn't done as well, but I did have one piece that aroused my curiosity. It was a chipped piece of jade with an edge that looked like it had been hit from both sides to sharpen it. When held so that the sharp edge could be used as a scraper, the piece felt good in the hand.

I said, "Look, this University of California guy never mentioned any jade touchstones, yet he must have dug up about half of a hundred-foot diameter shell mound at Willow Creek. In some places he went down five feet. He said they didn't fashion jade as tools, but look at this." I ran the scraper along the table, then tossed it to Jim.

Gary got out another piece. "Look at this one. It's a perfect trading piece. The guy's nuts. And we only dug about one cubic foot of shell mound."

"They must have valued it—traded it with the other Indians," Jim suggested.

Later that night as Jim and I were lying in our sleeping bags I remembered something else I had read. The local Indians believed that in the beginning all the lands of the earth were under the sea, except the very top of one mountain. An eagle, a coyote, and a kingfisher were on this mountain. Perhaps the eagle represented the air, the coyote land, and the kingfisher a joining of air, land, and water. These three animals created man, and then the earth, brought up from the primeval water for man, was given shape as it is today. This story fit in with the theories of the geological origin of the coastal ranges. The Indians also thought the souls of their dead inhabited a western island out in the ocean.

I thought of the time during the succession of glacial periods when Jade Cove must have been bare of sea. As recently as 10,000 years ago ancestors of these same coastal Indians might have sheltered themselves from storms within the green walls of the Cave Rock and might have buried their dead far to the west of the present shoreline. I remembered diving off La Jolla in southern California for Indian artifacts from Ice Age burial grounds said to have existed down to 60 feet below the current water level.

Jim must have been thinking about some of the same things. "You know, Don, some day we ought to come back down here just to study the Indians."

I thought about the Indians and us digging in the shell mounds, and I thought about Hank's gold, and the cave on the hill, and the geologic formation of the area, and I thought about jade.

"Jim, it's funny but everything about this country has mystery to it; everything down here is unsolved."

Jim didn't reply.

17. CLEANING UP

THE SEAS came up high and heavy that night, but by the next day it was calm again. A low tide in the morning revealed to us what rough seas can do to a beach. We looked at the stretch we had cleared the day before at Willow Creek, and a good hundred yards of what had been sand was now heavy with boulders. The surf had moved more sand and boulders within eight hours than all the rockhounds in the state could have moved in a month.

Gary went back to his new job, so Jim and I dove. But Jim got sick as soon as he got out in the water.

I finished his tank and four tanks of my own that day. I chipped the ledge some, then reset the cable and pulled the *Nephripod* about a quarter of an inch away from the Cave Rock. Then I reset the cable again and pulled in a slightly different direction. I made little progress toward the Gravel Pit, and the *Nephripod* didn't drop down.

That night it came to me that I should reset the cable again to pull at a slightly different angle, down the line of the south edge of the Cave Rock.

Resetting the cable was a big job. Rocks that were large enough so they would not be pulled toward the *Nephripod* had to be selected, and we had to make sure the cable wouldn't bind under the rocks or twist and get a permanent kink. We had to readjust the griphoist. Since there were usually small pieces of gravel in it, getting it into neutral and then back into gear was a test of strength. Usually it took a full tank or more of air just to reset the cable. Then as the cable was tightened by the griphoist it had to be inspected continually for binding and kinking and had to be tightened so that the cable rode on the wheels of the snatch block. If it got off a wheel it could bind and destroy the snatch block. Many times we had to disassemble the whole set-up and take the snatch block to shore to beat it back into shape.

The next day I set up the griphoist and pulled on the *Nephripod*. I put a terrific strain on it, but I was still working at a slightly wrong angle. First I broke a hook. Then I re-rigged and broke the high-tension chain. I decided to wrap the chain around the rock twice, reset the cable, and pull from the right angle.

I had been doing a lot of diving by myself. One day I discovered that I was talking out loud, but since I had my regulator mouthpiece clenched between my teeth my words came out rather jumbled. I don't remember just when it began, but I found myself talking to an imaginary character underwater.

As I was working on the griphoist I would say, "O.K., James, this time we're going to get it!"

Or, "Let's reset the cable; what do you think, James?"

It was a funny thing, but this underwater James character never once disagreed with me. A pleasant sort of fellow.

Back on the beach I said to Jim, "That rock sure is a stubborn bastard."

"You're just as stubborn," Jim shot back.

I began to think that the more stubborn the rock seemed the more determined I was to get it.

Sonny returned. By that time he and I were working very well together as a team. With the doubled chain we pulled from the new angle, putting a terrific strain on it. Now we saw that where the *Nephripod* grated against the ledge the jade rock was chipping the surface layer. Sonny got down on the sand and put his shoulder under the bar so that by using his legs he could lift the griphoist handle with his whole body. I propped my feet up on the face of the *Nephripod* and put my shoulder on the handle from the opposite direction using my whole body too. At last, when we were on our fourth and last tank, the jade broke loose! From then on one diver could move the rock with the griphoist by himself!

We were so happy about breaking the jade loose that we arrived in camp that evening blowing the horn and shouting. To give ourselves a special treat we had dinner in the combination service station-grocery-cafe that made up the entire settlement of Pacific Valley.

Jim had not felt well earlier in the day, and by the time dinner was over he felt so bad that he decided to phone Dr. Joe, a friend in Gilroy. I drove him the 90 miles to the doctor. He was so sick he slept in the back of the VW all the way.

The next day instead of working on the *Nephripod* I decided to see if I could pull out a 350 pound rock I had found while resetting the cable. Two lifting bags raised the rock easily. When I got it to the beach Gary and I worked it across the gravel and into the rocks, skidding it on a cushion of rotting algae. In the meantime Sonny went home to get some boards and a hand truck, and when he returned the three of us started dragging the rock up the stairs. Sonny straddled the rock and lifted while Gary and I pulled with the rope. We tried the hand truck, but it twisted in our hands on the rough terrain and threw me across the rocks. On the trail we counted "one, two, three" and pulled on the three count, skidding the rock along on top of some boards. The rock went ahead slowly, and I kept falling into the poison oak. We finally dumped the rock into the VW camper as the sun was setting.

I went back to school in San Francisco for a few days, scratching my legs.

By May 9 Jim had recovered from the flu, and he and I brought the jade trailer with the sled on it down to Jade Cove.

I dove to move some rocks away from the front of the *Nephripod,* using a crowbar. One large rock was loose but would need to be rolled or turned before the sled could be used, and it was a two-man job. As I was straining to move it Ernie swam out of nowhere to help me.

After the *Nephripod* had been pulled out from the Cave Rock a few inches the sand and gravel shifted away on the Cave Rock side, revealing several boulders. Sonny spotted one of them as another jade boulder. It was far under the overhang of the Cave Rock, about five feet in. We would have to wait until the *Nephripod* was lifted to get at it.

Back at camp I made a list of the rocks we had taken and those we planned to take:

1) The Green Pickle, 600 pounds (Jim's, taken).
2) Rock on cable line, 350 pounds (mine, taken).
3) Rock behind the *Nephripod,* 500 pounds (mine, to be taken).
4) Rock under the Cave Rock, 500 pounds (Sonny's, to be taken).
5) *The Nephripod* (ours, to be taken).

We now dug gingerly more than an arm's length under the *Nephripod,* all along the eight-foot side. As far as we could tell, the whole bottom of the rock was flat. This was a break. The *Nephripod* had dropped, but very slightly, so we decided that if the edge of the sled could be pushed under the rock a couple of feet it would slide onto the sled when we pulled it, clearing the overhanging ledge.

Now, at last, we were ready to go on to the next phase of *Project Nephripod:* the sled and the lift!

18. THE SLED

THE NEXT DAY, May 10, Gary and Sonny arrived. We had planned to put the sled in the ocean at Willow Creek Cove, but there was a high surf. We considered lowering or carrying it down the cliff at Jade Cove, but since it weighed 500 pounds we decided this would be dangerous and might damage the trail. Mill Creek was a long way from the Cove by sea, but we could get close to the beach from the road and the surf was fairly calm. So we decided to launch it there.

The day was sunny with a slight breeze. Though the surf was low an occasional boomer hit the south end beach, so we went to the north end. We moved the Speedyak to the beach, then dragged the sled down a slight bluff, finally attaching chains and pulling on them to haul the sled to the surf line.

Jim and Gary were elected to haul the sled to Jade Cove. We chained two barrels to the sled and tied them together across the top so they wouldn't bang. Then Sonny and I launched the Speedyak. The tow rope ran back to the sled on shore, and we pulled as Jim and Gary edged the sled through the surf. Sonny and I escorted the Speedyak out a ways, then swam back to shore. We were going to meet them at the Cove.

We changed into dry clothes and got into the VW to follow their erratic voyage along the coast. It looked as though the sea was coming up. Jim and Gary were out beyond the kelp beds, and whitecaps pocked the surface clear to the horizon. Progress seemed slow. The sea continued to roughen and since both voyagers were prone to seasickness we speculated that by now they were probably sick and miserable.

We decided to keep a close eye on them rather than go to the Cove. After two hours they still hadn't made much progress. Thinking that they might run out of gas and have to put in to shore, we found a cove where, if worse came to worst, they could bring in the gear for the night. It was a small, sheltered beach north of Pacific Valley Store where to the shoreward of some jagged offshore rocks the water remained relatively calm. Sonny suited up for a long swim out, so that he could guide them in through the offshore rocks. But we noticed they were going by and not going to put in to shore.

I said to Sonny, "What the hell; we can't help them. Let's have a beer and think about it."

At Pacific Valley Store we sat near the big window enjoying the panoramic sweep of the coast. We could barely make out two tiny spots on the ocean. The store manager asked us what we were staring at.

I said, "See those two damn fools way out there in that rough water, those two little black specks? That's Jim and Gary. That's us, our team, bringing a sled with equipment on it down to Jade Cove. I don't know why they picked such a rough day to work. They must be out of their skulls! Let's have another beer."

But they were making progress, and soon they rounded the point and dropped behind Plaskett Rock. It was time for us to stop toasting them.

We suited up and climbed down the cliff. Ten hours from the time when we had pulled and shoved the sled through the surf at Mill Creek they pulled into the Cove.

Sonny and I unscrewed both plug and bung from each barrel, and the sled sank down to the Gravel Pit below. Underwater, we detached the two empty barrels from the sled, put the plugs in, and blew air into the barrels through the bung-holes. At the surface we replaced the bungs and swam the barrels ashore. Jim and Gary were tired from their long day. I was feeling sorry for Jim; he looked beat. At the same time I was glad that Gary and not I had been with him. What we had thought would be a lark had turned into a nightmare trip. They even had a whale shake them up as it surfaced and spouted dangerously close to the Speedyak.

That night as we lay in our sleeping bags talking, Jim sounded tired and discouraged. "I had to choke the Seagull all the way part of the time, then unchoke it the rest of the time. But most of the time I had to hold it in just one position and, hell, between holding one finger on the choke and the other on the handle, and steering, correcting.... With those waves I had to correct it all the way."

"We could see the waves coming up from the shore," I said. "They looked pretty spotty, like they were breaking all over the ocean."

"They were pretty high, Don. We were going up and down, and then we would get into sort of a choppy place ... the waves very close together. It wasn't so much choppy; it's just that we were so damned close to the sled. And the rope would jerk."

"You really let the rope out after a while, though. We could see from shore."

"We let it out to better than 125 feet so it wouldn't jerk so much."

"We ought to have those snubbers, huh?"

"No, the tow rope was much better than snubbers. It's nylon and it stretches. The rope was a heck of a good thing, and it ... it will be good when we bring in the Big Jade too. Because we can tie the little line to that rope, and that rope is pretty long." Jim yawned.

"You think that using two boats is a good way to haul the Big Jade?"

"Yes, I think so. The question is whether we're going to have enough guys to handle two boats and do all the work that has to be done. If we have a nice quiet day one boat should be all right, and maybe one guy in one boat."

"Yeah. Of course the run down to Willow Creek isn't as bad as the one you had today. It's not that far."

"No. It's about one-third, maybe a fourth less. But, Don, I just think that the kelp is getting thicker."

"Yeah, it's getting bad."

"God, it's really thick in spots."

"Yeah."

After a silence Jim's voice seemed to come from a long way off. "I don't know how it's going to be, getting the *Nephripod* down to the Creek. I guess we'll just have to do it, you know, before the kelp gets much worse."

As I lay there I thought of how fast kelp grows and how difficult it can be to get through. I could see us stuck, our Big Jade caught in a Sargasso sea of entanglement, unable to move. I visualized the rock suspended just beneath the surface and Sonny and I underwater with large knives, cutting the kelp around the rock strand by strand. But it was a nice vision, seeing the rock suspended, slowly rocking as it edged through the dense growth on its way toward Willow Creek. It seemed a warm and comfortable thought, and I tried to hang onto the image for a long time, as if the image of it would somehow make it happen. By the time the rock was raised most of my worries would be over. If it took us a week to get it down to Willow, so what? So what's a little kelp? As I dropped off to sleep I decided that Jim worried too much.

19. JADE ON THE SLED

THE NEXT DAY when Sonny and I finished our first dive fresh tanks were ready for us. By the time we had finished our second dive Jim was on his way to Cayucos to hide the jade trailer at Sonny's sister's house until we needed it and to rent more tanks and refill the empties. That day we used four tanks apiece.

First we moved rocks and set the sled in place, sliding one edge of it about a foot under the shoreward edge of the *Nephripod*. Then we pumped on the rock with the griphoist. Until that time we had only moved it about three inches in all, but now we moved it a full six inches in less than five minutes. As the rock began to move over the sled it shifted upwards and started binding under the ledge again. Why wouldn't it drop? We chipped on the ledge again with the sharp end of the crowbar in an attempt to bring the *Nephripod* through.

On shore, between tanks, we agreed that we would try to bully the *Nephripod* through, pumping like hell on the griphoist in hopes that our rock would eventually push down under the ledge and clear itself.

So again Sonny got under one side of the griphoist handle and pushed up with his shoulder, while I got on the opposite side with my feet up on the *Nephripod* and pushed down with my shoulder. Occasionally I quit pumping and used the crowbar to help chip the ledge in a specific spot.

Once again we strained so hard that from time to time we had to go to the surface. Above water we draped our arms over the edge of the float to rest and get our breathing back to normal and renewed our resolve to muscle the *Nephripod* through.

At last, the Big Jade began cracking through the surface jade of the ledge as it moved onto the sled. Finally it broke free!

Now we began to put it on the sled. To move the *Nephripod* into position we moved the griphoist to the other side of the rock to swing it around, but then we discovered we could actually move one end of it with the crowbar. We finally got it on the sled. As I was putting the chain net over it I caressed the back side of the rock that I had only glimpsed before and whistled as best I could underwater. It was beautiful!

We had trouble with shackles and had to use two in some places, because the links in the high-tensile-strength chain were too small to shove the shackles through. But soon we had the chain net over it and the rock was ready to lift! On our last tank we attached more clevises around the perimeter of the sled to fasten to the chains on the barrels. Then we moved additional rocks away from the edge so the barrels would fit snugly. By the end of the day we had the griphoist attached to a large rock that was too close. Besides that one there was only one other large rock to move.

We wondered if we shouldn't take out the smaller jade rocks before we raised the *Nephripod* because weekend divers might try to take them. On the other hand, we felt it would be wise to remove the *Nephripod* before the weekenders saw our project. As a compromise we decided we would tie the small jade in nets so other divers would see it was staked out and would leave it alone.

That night in the house trailer we celebrated our progress. It was dark outside when we lit the candle. The wine came out, followed by cheese and crackers. In the warm half-light we discussed what had to be done the next day in preparation for the big move. We had to do some coordinating—had to get the Seagull motor and all the towing equipment ready and also the shore gear that would be used to haul the rock in and up onto the beach at Willow Creek.

We decided that Jim would stay in camp and organize the equipment. Gary would help portage tanks and other gear down the cliff, while Sonny and I did final clean-up work around the sled. We still had to move those two large rocks to get the barrels in close so the load would ride high.

The pressure was on. Now that the rock was chained we decided to move it out before the weekend—which meant we would have to forget about the smaller stones. The Big Jade was the important thing. If we could take the remaining barrels down the cliff, clear the old chain off the rock, move the nearby rocks away, and fasten all the barrels and some lifting bags on the rock, then we could lift the *Nephripod* on the second morning.

We had to figure the tides. Once we started, everything had to go just right; there would be no second chance. The tide would be high at two in the afternoon and the rock would have to come through the surf close to that time so it would be high and dry at low tide the following morning.

By the end of the next day we were ready for the big lift. All the barrels were on and fastened down with shackles, except some of the center chains that were difficult to get at. The barrels were bound together with line so they wouldn't bang each other to pieces in the surge during the night. We removed the griphoist, cable, extra chain, and all other miscellaneous gear from the site and carried it up the cliff.

Then we made a mistake that was to cost us dearly. We had carried about 20 lifting bags down to the beach during the day and then decided not to put them on the rock until the next day. Since it was sunset and we were exhausted from our trips up and down the trail, we decided to leave the bags on the beach. Ceremoniously, I folded my socks across the top of the pile of bags, and we headed up the trail for the last time that day.

20. THE LIFT

WE WANTED to try to lift the rock while our full crew of four was on hand, even though the ocean was not completely calm. Gary and I went to Pacific Valley and telephoned some of our friends at the Moss Landing Marine Laboratory, near Monterey. Since it was possible that we might have problems bringing the *Nephripod* through the Willow Creek surf we wanted to have some more divers on hand. We discovered that Moss Landing was having Open House that Sunday, so a handful of students promised to cut classes and help us, on the supposition that if we got our rock out on time we could show it at their Open House. We told them that we would make their Open House an event that wouldn't be soon forgotten, because we were going to bring in the biggest piece of jade on the continent. (This was the first time we admitted to outsiders how large the *Nephripod* was.)

Sonny, at his sister's in Cambria for the night, had all the diving tanks filled, and by the time Gary and I got back to camp he was back with his sister's boyfriend, Carl. Although Carl had never handled a 16 mm movie camera, he was to be the official cameraman to document the raising of the *Nephripod*.

On my first trip down to the Cove I thought of the lifting bags we had left on the beach overnight, and how Gary, with his faith in people, had assured me no one would steal them, insinuating that I was a little uptight about the roving hippies on the coast. I had protested, "Well, they're our life's blood. We shouldn't leave them on the beach." But the final decision had been mine.

Much to my relief they were still there, as were the socks which I had folded neatly across them.

Sonny and I suited up to dive. Gary went up and down the trail, hauling air tanks to fill the lifting bags with. Jim's job was to take the tanks and the lifting bags out to us in the Speedyak.

Underwater, Sonny and I removed the ropes from the barrels so that each one swung free on its chains. We put a small valve on each barrel which could be fastened to a filling hose on an air tank. Sonny filled barrels while I went around with short ropes, and when a barrel became buoyant I reached under it tying the center chain to the sled. Now all the chains on the barrels we had not been able to reach with shackles were secured with rope. The barrels filled easily.

Sonny and I then surfaced and brought the lifting bags down six at a time, hooking them onto the chain network which covered the *Nephripod*. We blew air into each of the six bags, partially filling them, then went up for more.

When most of the bags were filled to capacity the sled began shifting slowly back and forth, banging into rocks. Sonny and I went up for more bags. Jim handed us five and said they were the last. We put five bags on and inflated them.

I couldn't believe what was happening. We had used all the bags, and still our rock would not lift! I swam up to talk to Jim again, and he said that there were definitely no more bags.

Sonny had run out of air and gone ashore for another tank. Soon my tank ran out too and I had to swim for shore, leaving the lifting gear banging back and forth on the sled that was now moving with the surge. On my way in I passed Sonny, who was on his way back with a fresh tank. He said that since the surge appeared to be increasing he should let enough air out of the bags to let the rock settle down again. I agreed, but knowing how much work it is to let air out of full bags I did not envy him his task.

When I got to shore I found that Gary was talking to four Moss Landing students who had come to help us. I should have been happy to see them, but since my anxiety about the rock was mounting I greeted them brusquely.

I shouted to Jim, asking him if he was sure there were no more lifting bags, not even in camp.

"No."

No? I didn't believe it.

I had begun to sweat inside my suit, and sweat was dripping off my nose. I tried to work it out in my mind: "Let's see, if there are no more lifting bags on shore or in camp, then we can't lift the rock." It seemed discouragingly simple.

But how could that be? Jim and I had gone over and over the lifting capacity of our gear time and time again. I thought we had a good safety margin. There must be bags in someone's car, in the trailer, somewhere. Surely someone must have overlooked them somehow.

Suddenly it seemed as though time were standing still. No one but me seemed to be concerned that our equipment was out there getting torn to pieces beneath the sea. Who knew what trouble Sonny might now be in? It was unnerving not knowing what was going on, seeing nothing happen. Even while we were standing around on the beach doing nothing, the surf was coming up, and the equipment was getting pounded to bits. Yet, no one was moving.

Desperately, I interrupted Gary. "Did we get every last lifting bag? Are there more in camp? Anywhere?

Gary seemed oblivious to the problem. "Oh no, we didn't use them all. There are more on shore. You remember, the ones we left overnight."

We hadn't told Jim about them, but I couldn't believe that Gary hadn't given them to him to take out to us. I was hot and felt dizzy. It was too much like a bad dream. Then I got mad. I screamed for everyone to get on it, that we were going to lose the whole goddamn thing if we didn't get off our duffs.

Things began to happen. I got a new tank and Gary got the lifting bags that had been forgotten and another "fill" tank and got in the Speedyak with Jim. We were organized once more.

When we got back to the site Sonny and I took some of the bags down and discovered, much to our dismay, that while the bags were intact someone had cut the clips off each one of them. We surfaced again. Where the clips should have been there were only severed ends of nylon rope. Whoever had taken the clips must have restacked the bags and even replaced my socks, being careful to fold them back as I had them before.

It was sabotage! I was even more frantic than before. We decided to quick-tie the ends of the severed rope together and then fasten two bags to a clip, which would seem to be an easy thing to do. I went down to try it out and discovered that the extra bag put a sideways strain on the clip that would break it, which would then cause us to lose both bags. We had no choice but to untie all the knots, then try to tie the bags on underwater with the short ropes.

At last we were filling the bags that should take the *Nephripod* up. This was the moment we had been working toward all winter.

The huge stone was bound like a lifeless corpse, like some dead Gulliver, beneath its net of high-tensile strength chain. Now our lifting equipment began to give it life as we added air to the last of the bags. Suddenly it gave a shudder and we could feel it shift beneath our hands, ever so slightly, moving with the surge. Our sleeping giant was awakening.

The huge gem was still on the bottom, but as the sled pivoted on its heaviest corner the three other corners rose from the sand. Then we could no longer hold it. The whole sled swung, pivoting around the low point, sweeping in an erratic semicircle and then back again like a giant scythe, taking everything in its path with it. As the burden lightened more the sled began to travel back and forth with the surge, lunging shoreward, pounding against large rocks, pausing and then moving back again, and chipping or crushing smaller ones. It swept along like some awesome battering ram, taking us with it. We moved cautiously, trying to keep our fins and limbs out of the way, all the while furiously tying on and filling additional bags. Whenever possible we worked above the rock, reaching down among the bags that were already on it to tie on new bags where they would balance the tilted sled and enable the load to rise evenly. And always there was the fear that the surrounding rocks would tear off some of the bags or poke a hole in a barrel. We seemed to be creating an uncontrollable monster with each puff of air.

I had lost track of the fact that the *Nephripod* was traveling along the bottom and taking me with it, and as I reached over a barrel to fill a bag the sled shifted toward me, dragging me backward and pinning me against the ledge. I put my hands against the barrel instinctively, but it knocked the wind from my chest and kept coming. I was squashed against the ledge. I pushed against the barrel, straining, but there was no way I could resist such weight. Then the surge suddenly changed directions and the sled moved away. I got out fast.

I was afraid that before it was raised to the surface the whole mass might get loose and move out into the Gravel Pit. If that happened it would probably be thrust fifteen to twenty feet one way and then back with the surge, just as we had been tossed about by the heavy surges of midwinter. The tremendous force of all that weight banging up against the Cave Rock could shatter barrels and tear bags, ruining our equipment in short order. Even confined by surrounding rocks it was making three-to-four-foot lunges, and the barrels had already taken sizable dents.

We had agreed that when I thought the rock was ready to be raised I would yank three times on the tow rope. When Jim got my message up above in the Speedyak he was to start the Seagull and start pulling the rock to seaward to keep it from crashing against the Cave Rock as it rose. When he felt the rope jerk he was to raise his hand as a signal to Carl, who was up on the cliffs with the movie camera. Carl would then get set to film the *Nephripod* as it broke the surface.

Sonny was still putting air in bags. I planted my fins on the ocean floor, grabbed the lowest corner of the sled, and found that I could raise it. I tapped Sonny on the shoulder. He looked up at me, and I signaled that we should try to lift the sled. We got on opposite corners, nodded to each other, then lifted. Straining, we brought the sled swiftly to shoulder height. It was still moving back and forth with the surge. Then all of a sudden the air in the bags expanded enough to lift it, and we felt it leave our hands and move upward—out of control! At first it moved slowly, then gained momentum. It careened against the Cave Rock, which overhung on one side above us, but kept on going. It was hurtling unsteadily, drunkenly, toward an uncertain birth above.

It is hard to say what feelings one has when things are moving so fast, or how time may work to distort your image of them. But that lift is engraved upon my mind. I can close my eyes and see the sled rising, see how the light filtering through the canopy of kelp above came down around it like a halo of bright spokes. I can still see a corner of the sled hurtling against the overhang and the shattering of whatever it scraped against on its way up. I can trace indelibly its final, agonizing route to the surface and feel again, as though I were there, my fear that equipment would be damaged on the way up and that the Nephripod would come tumbling back down on top of us.

Sonny and I followed it up, swimming fast, for it hung suspended in the water above us. When we surfaced we emerged from a silent, muffled cocoon of water into a different world, a world with a wild and obscenely noise-filled atmosphere that demanded immediate answers.

Gary and Jim were shouting. Jim was struggling with the Seagull, which he couldn't start.

The whole Cove was white with foam. Waves were knocking the Big Jade against the Cave Rock. I was suddenly panicky. Any instant now the barrels might be pounded to bits and the jade would go down again. It felt like an eternity before Sonny and I realized that we could at least try to hold the sled away from the Cave Rock. We saw the tow rope just beneath our fins, dove for it, and started to pull.

About that time we heard the Seagull start and Jim throw it in gear. We felt the line go taut in our hands. Slowly, slowly, the Big Jade moved away from the Cave Rock. The little inflatable boat was actually pulling it!

We had done it! Now for the long trip to Willow Creek, and the rock was ours!

Sonny and I did some frantic, last minute chores as the rock moved slowly seaward. Sonny put bungs in the barrels to make them air-tight. I found a bag which had torn loose, then another. Jim gave me some line and I retied and inflated both bags. Then Sonny and I swam around the rock and filled each bag we could reach with as much air as it would take. Thin streams of bubbles were rising from some of the bags, and one of the smaller ones was leaking heavily.

It was a long swim back to the beach for Sonny and me. Just before passing the Cave Rock we turned and looked seaward and saw Jim and Gary in the Speedyak on the crest of a swell, behind them a low black island of bags. To me, there seemed to be only a four- or five-bag margin showing above water. While a five-bag margin equaled a 1,000 pound safety factor, the loss of only five bags would be catastrophic. Also, there were large ground swells, and each time the rock slid to the bottom of a trough the force of all that weight pulling down on the bags would result in increased water pressure, decreasing the volume of air within each bag and causing a loss of buoyancy. I looked at the rising sea and felt a fresh west wind blowing cold on my face.

Sonny shook his head. "I don't think they're going to make it!"

21. LOST AT SEA

ASHORE, recalling my recent screaming and shouting, I apologized to the four students from Moss Landing, hoping that they would understand. They helped carry the equipment up the cliff. Two of the students agreed to meet us at Willow Creek but the other two decided to go back to Moss Landing. Carl, who had finished photographing for the moment, went to pick up some lunch.

As Sonny and I drove toward Willow Creek we could see the Speedyak out to sea, still towing its island of lifting bags. We stopped on a cliff and looked down at the water. They were like specks on the vast surface of the ocean, first coming in toward shore, then carefully threading their way between meadows of kelp. They rose and fell with each swell, but they seemed to be making good time. It looked as if they were going to make it!

At Willow Creek I took the cable, snatch block and extra line to the south beach and hooked it to a large rock that would serve as a deadman. The sandwiches arrived, but I was too excited to eat.

Garrison and Lindquist, the two Moss Landing students, arrived too and prepared to lend a hand in the water—a gesture I welcomed, even though they had dipped into the Red Mountain wine. Once they hit the cool Pacific, they would sober up fast. They had two hippie hitchhikers with them. One of them was stoned out of his mind and kept falling down in the sand, jouncing around, laughing and saying, "Is this jade? Wow, really far out!" and the usual stock hippie phrases. The other one, who was reasonably coherent, was to remain on the beach and pull the jade in while the rest of us guided it through the water.

Finally, we saw the one-ship flotilla rounding the point, fighting the heavy swells. The Speedyak was a tiny white speck among the whitecaps, trailing a small black island behind. Then both of them sank down into a trough, and it was a long time before we found them again.

Concerned with getting our divers ready, I suited up once more, still nervous and excited. Sonny climbed up the cliff behind us to get a better view. Suddenly he shouted, "I don't see them anywhere!" We all squinted seaward. No one could see them any more. They were gone!

Sonny and I leaped into the VW. We didn't expect a disaster, but we thought that since they should be near soon we had better pinpoint them so our divers could get out to them. Time was growing short.

I raced the VW up the steep Willow Creek grade. After a brief but vain scan of the sea in front of Willow Creek I skidded the VW out into the highway, heading north. I finally pulled over on a bluff halfway to Jade Cove, jerking the car to a halt. We burst out and ran toward the sea. There was no sign of them.

We ran along the bluffs to better see the beaches below, thinking of all sorts of possibilities. The transom might have torn out of the Speedyak and they might be swimming for shore and be hard to spot in the rough water. Or they might have sunk and could be trapped on an isolated beach below. It was impossible to check out all the surf and beaches from the cliffs. Maybe the rock had sunk, dragging them down tangled in the rope....

I prayed, "Dear God, please save those two big lunks from the sea." I even bargained: "... and I don't give a damn about that rock!" My prayer was more like an oath. I could see Jim sinking down into the green kelp, lashed to the rock in a tangle of rope, his eyes bulging out—down to his doom. I could hear his last anguished cry and envisioned the world suddenly dumb, emptied of both him and Gary, the sea, now grey and sickly, closing over them forever.

But what could Sonny and I do? How could we help?

It seemed foolish, but we decided to go back to Jade Cove. Once there, we hurdled the stile and ran down the meadow to the top of the cliff.

Jim and Gary were below in the Speedyak! Thank God! They put up the motor and were rowing in slowly through the kelp past the Cave Rock. But there was no sign of the *Nephripod!* For the moment that didn't matter. We were glad that they were safe. We ran down the trail to the beach.

The *Nephripod* had gone down in a trough after a high swell. They had left the tow rope on it with a plastic Clorox bottle as buoy, then cut themselves loose. Gary said that the last they saw of the buoy it looked as if the *Nephripod* was drifting out to sea.

There was nothing we could do. We had lost our jade, and months of work, and more than a few dollars worth of equipment. I could picture the giant rock drifting out to sea just beneath the surface of the water and a Navy destroyer ploughing into it, sinking the destroyer.

Later I realized that when the rock started sinking it would gain weight at a tremendous rate. The air in the lifting bags would compress, and the barrels would implode. At 30 feet deep our 8,000 pound rock would weigh as much as a 4,000 pound rock without flotation would weigh at the surface. There was no way such a weight could drift with any current. The rock would lie below where it was cut loose. Our only problems, then, were to locate the site where it went down and to find out how deep it sank.

We carried the Speedyak and motor up the cliff. Jim and Gary went back to camp, and Sonny and I went to Willow Creek with the bad news.

I thanked Garrison and Lindquist as they prepared to leave for Moss Landing.

In parting, Garrison said fondly, "You really blew it this time, Wobber."

"Yeah, I blew it."

I thought of the students at the Open House, and Garrison telling them what had happened to their Big Jade exhibit. I remembered how mad I had been on the beach, then how apologetic and grateful for their help, then how excited I was in anticipation of landing the rock at Willow Creek. Jim and I had lifted our rock, all right, but we had let it slip through our fingers. What tales would Garrison tell about the two old fools who had failed in their efforts to beach their great *Nephripod?*

"Oh well, it was only a rock," I offered blankly.

"Sure," Garrison said as he put his car in gear and drove off.

22. PROBLEMS

SONNY AND I slowly gathered the remaining gear. Then we drove north, searching the ocean as we went. After twenty minutes we finally made out a small white dot—the clorox bottle forlornly bobbing up and down in the fading sunlight. We triangulated on it and went back to camp.

"Christ, I still can't believe it!" I said, pouring myself some cheap German wine. As I swirled the wine around in the glass I thought of the months of labor we had spent on this godforsaken coast. "You guys were *so* close."

"Yes, we were close. And we'd have made it too, if those bags had only had clips."

I felt helpless. The four of us sat around the table, the pressure cooker rattling, as we had so often sat before—but it had never been like this. I put my glass down in front of me and stared into the urine-colored liquid. My hands felt awkward and I felt empty and cramped in the small trailer.

"You know what bugs me is that now the word is out," I said. "Now the Moss Landing crowd knows how big the rock is. And they know we lost it...."

"And they know *where* we lost it."

"Oh, I'm not worried about that part. We can trust those guys."

"They know about it down in Cambria too," Sonny said, "and in Morro Bay. Those guys down there are all talking. The rock shops, Lonnie and Walter, they spread the word. Everyone down there is excited."

"Jesus Christ!"

Garrison's words came back to me: "You really blew it this time, Wobber."

Jim said, "We might have other problems too. The kelp's still growing. It's getting thick. We could also have problems with the rangers."

"What do you mean? They all knew we were going to do it. They just thought it was a smaller rock. There won't be any trouble with them."

"Well, remember what happened with Big Thumper? People got excited...." Big Thumper was a 2,400 pound rock we had beached in 1963.

"Yeah, that was something." I explained to Gary and Sonny: "We were floating this rock into Willow. We had six guys working on it and all kinds of problems. Well, word got around the campground, and up and down the coast, and by the time we got it to Willow there were about 50 spectators on the shore. And among them, just as big as life, was this frigging U.S. of A. Forest Ranger, standing there about ten feet tall with his hands on his hips, looking us over.

"Perry and I were out on the rock paddling it in. Perry said, 'What do we do now?' I said, 'I don't know. We're not breaking any laws, but just in case we are, we've had our fun, so why should we worry if they take our rock and slap us in jail? Be a new experience.' But I was really scared. Then the ranger got in his truck and we saw him heading north up the Coast Highway. I figured he went to get more rangers, because there were six of us and the crowd on the beach might have taken our side. He might have had a riot on his hands."

"But he never came back."

"Yes, but what we didn't know then was that when he was standing on the beach in the crowd he turned to Perry's wife and said, 'Those guys have spent so much time and worked so hard for that rock, I'm not going to be the one to take it away from them.' Then he left."

"That ranger turned out to be Ralph Gould. We got to know him later. He's one of the nicest guys going."

"Ralph told us later about some bitchy old lady who was probably going through the change busting into his office complaining about us stealing jade. She demanded that he go down and stop us, and she wanted him to call the sheriff. Now that everybody knows about the *Nephripod* the same thing could happen again."

"Yeah, or other divers might try to get the jade now that it's out in the open and easy to get at. Now that they know we lost it they'll be down here thick as flies trying to get it."

After dinner Jim and I talked into the wee hours, mostly about how we would try to re-rig the rock to lift it again—if it wasn't too deep; deep water might make recovery impossible.

Gary had to get back to his job, so he left early the next morning. Sonny dove near the Cave Rock to work on the smaller jade rock we had found.

Jim and I headed out in the Speedyak to where the *Nephripod* had gone down. Our concern was how deep it lay. Jim was sure that it was not over 40 feet down. I thought it would be much deeper and could picture it at 120 feet, completely out of reach.

We spotted the clorox buoy easily, even though heavy swells were running. The water looked clear. If the jade was only 30 to 40 feet down we should be able to see it from the surface in clear water. I looked down and saw nothing but blue and the tow rope disappearing out of sight. I pulled on the rope. It was straight and heavy; it felt as though I were raising the length of chain to which it was attached. I thought the rope must be on the bottom and the rock in 175 feet of water, and my heart sank. We could never recover it from that depth.

I pulled the rope tight, and to my relief I was able to pull some rope into the Speedyak. The weight of the wet rope had made it feel heavy and had held it down. I kept pulling, bringing in rope, feeling better and better as more of it came aboard. When the rope was finally taut Jim put a knot in it so that we could measure it when we got to camp to gauge the water's depth. (Unfortunately, we lost track of which end was attached to the sled, so we weren't able to tell whether the rock was at 55 feet or 70 feet.)

I suited up and went in. When I got down to 30 feet I could see the *Nephripod* below, cocked at a 30-degree angle, resting on some huge rocks. All the barrels had imploded.

I went up and Jim handed me the chain cutter; then I dove and cut one barrel off and swam up with it. It was so crumpled it was not worth salvaging. I went down again and took off a lifting bag. I looked around for a place to clip it while I gathered more of them. I clipped the bag to the tow rope, then had an idea. I blew a little air in the bag and sent it up the tow rope. It rose like an elevator, slowly at first and then as the air expanded faster and faster until it disappeared out of sight. I wondered what Jim's reaction would be when he saw the first bag coming up, then the others.

When I had sent about ten bags to the surface I went up to see how Jim was getting along. He was busily gathering bags into the Speedyak, as if he were harvesting a school of large black fish. I dove again and sent up 19 bags in all. I replaced the mountain climbing rope with some lighter line and then, low on air, surfaced again.

Although we had other problems to think about, I felt enthusiastic once more as I dumped my tank into the Speedyak. Now that I had been down to see the *Nephripod* I knew that recovery was possible.

Jim was not quite as enthusiastic. In fact, he was feeling sick from the rolling ground swells. We quickly attached an eight-pound anchor to a rope and threw out a second marker buoy about 20 feet to the shoreward of the site. When we got underway Jim felt better. The lifting bags I had recovered plus my diving gear filled the Speedyak, so I perched on top of them. A seal appeared, playing around us as we churned along. He followed us all the way back to the Cove.

Later that afternoon at the top of the trail we put our gear down to take a rest. The sun on the horizon threw a million gleaming swords over the sea. We leaned against the rail, gazing down the coast.

Suddenly Jim yelled, "Killer whales!"

God almighty! There were three enormous killer whales circling right where Jim and I had been that morning. Their huge black triangular dorsal fins stuck out of the water like sails in mourning.

"Sure as hell, killer whales! And the *Nephripod* is right beneath them!"

23. PIRATES BY SEA

THE NEXT MORNING as I lay in my sleeping bag inside the trailer, thinking about how badly things had gone and of our months of work gone to waste, I could hear the breakers pounding on the shore. With the surf so rough there was no chance of getting the remaining lifting bags off the *Nephripod*. Remembering the killer whales, I decided that it was just as well. I got up, had breakfast, slipped quietly from the trailer and started on my long drive home, leaving Jim and Sonny behind. I planned to return to the Cove after school was out.

At home I cleaned and stored my diving gear, got out my school books and prepared to devote myself to final exams.

I was making progress on my first morning home when I got a frantic call from Jim.

"Some guys from Morro Bay are trying to pirate our rock," he said.

At first I thought he might have made the story up. I felt exasperated. "Well, what do you want me to do? Come down there?"

Jim hesitated. "No, I guess we can handle it. We'll keep in touch."

I was relieved. I thought he was going to say yes. Good old Jim....

"Sonny and I think it's the salvage boat *Corregidor* out of Morro Bay. It looks like they're going to put a hard-hat diver down, pick up the jade and haul it away."

Carl had told Sonny about the *Corregidor* group. He said he was approached to find out whether Sonny would be willing to leave us and join them in pirating the *Nephripod*. There was a rumor that they had a $40,000 cash offer for the rock, sight unseen.

I spoke to my lawyer, who recommended a marine lawyer, who said he would look into the rules and regulations. The next day the marine lawyer called back and said he couldn't come up with anything (he did come up with a bill for $85 however). A friend of Gary's who was a lawyer said that if the pirates kept our equipment on the jade we could follow them to port and have them placed under arrest. He suggested that we get in touch with the sheriff at Morro Bay who would arrest them when they got to port. We would be required to put up a bond of ten percent of the value of the jade, and if the pirates didn't come up with a lawyer within 24 hours the rock would be ours.

This relieved some of the pressure, and I tried to get back to my studies.

When Jim and I next talked he mentioned the possibility of hiring a boat and our friend Ernie Porter to do a fast salvage job on the rock. I didn't like the idea; it wasn't in the spirit of "doing things ourselves in our own way."

However, if it would save the rock from the pirates and if Ernie and Sonny could do the salvage I was willing to make a fast trip down and film the raising of the rock.

Jim and Ernie cased the boats in Morro Bay to get an idea of who the pirates might be. They even talked to the bookkeeper of the *Corregidor*. They told him they wanted to hire the boat for a salvage job, but the bookkeeper refused, saying that the *Corregidor* had no insurance to cover taking such a load that close in to the coast. And none of the other local boats were rigged to lift that sort of weight.

Carl, who seemed to have some inside information on the pirates, said that none of them were divers. He told us they wanted to buy Sonny off so he could pinpoint the location of the jade for them. Then they would bring in a commercial hard-hat diver and steal the rock.

Evidently, they didn't know Sonny. Sonny's solution to the pirates' threat was to sit on top of the cliff with a gun (which he did) and blast away at them if they got near the rock (which, fortunately, he never did.

When Jim later inspected Sonny's gun he said that if Sonny had ever pulled the trigger it would probably have blown up.)

We lived for the next month in constant fear that the pirates would materialize and we would have a fight either on the sea or in court. Each fishing boat or yacht sighted off the coast aroused our suspicions. We were afraid that at night or under the cover of fog they could put a diver down, raise the *Nephripod* with cranes and lifting bags, and then escape, towing our treasure away and leaving our markers riding on an empty sea.

24. LOST AND FOUND

IT HAD BEEN three weeks since we had last been on the site of the sunken *Nephripod,* since the day I removed the lifting bags. School was out for summer vacation.

Jim was in the hospital, afraid he would lose sight in one eye as a result of a virus infection. Although he had the best possible medical care, the doctors were pessimistic. One of them said the infection had produced incurable scar tissue behind the eye.

Before Jim left the Cove he asked Ernie Porter if he would help us. Ernie agreed and was to be paid on a day-to-day basis. I was happy to have him. We needed an extra diver, and Ernie seemed the best possible choice.

To raise the *Nephripod* from a 70-foot depth we would need seven tanks to lift it, plus three tanks apiece for Sonny, Ernie, and me, and extra tanks as a safety factor. The small Speedyak was not adequate to carry all the gear to the site, so I purchased a large Avon inflatable raft. Our plan was to leave one man, Gary, on the surface to make sure that the gear would not get loose and drift away.

Ernie showed up at Willow Creek at eleven o'clock. The Avon raft was completely full: the tanks on the bottom were all lined up, and the lifting bags and two large float bags in heavy rope nets which Ernie had brought were on top. We tied the barrels all in a line, strung together like the dead bodies in *The Cruel Sea.*

We launched the Speedyak with Gary in it, and while he stood offshore, keeping the Seagull motor going, Sonny swam through the surf with a line tied to the first barrel. Ernie and I put the others in the

water, advancing the whole lot one by one, and Sonny pulled them to the Speedyak. Three of us then moved the Avon with the remaining gear into the surf, and Ernie and I jumped on opposite sides and knelt, paddling frantically on an outgoing backwash while Sonny pulled us by the bow line. The Avon almost dumped, but luckily we just edged over a large breaker and were suddenly out of danger.

We rode out to where the *Nephripod* had sunk, two divers in the raft and two in the Speedyak. When we got there we found only one marker buoy.

Ernie dove, tracing the buoy line down. He returned almost immediately. "The jade isn't there!"

"Aw, you're kidding," I said.

"No, really. It isn't there."

In disbelief I dove down, following the line. On the bottom I found the eight-pound anchor—but no jade. I made a frantic circle around the anchor twice, scanning an area 30 feet wide as I swam. Only large boulders and sand, but no jade!

After my futile search the three of us used a tank of valuable air apiece in widening search patterns. There was no sign of the *Nephripod* anywhere.

Since we had triangulated the location only from the cliffs and not from the sea, I decided to go ashore to try to put one diver, Ernie, on the site. Then we would know for sure. Gary took me back to Willow Creek beach in the Speedyak and I dumped off just outside the breaker line and swam ashore as Gary returned to the others. Still dripping water from my wet suit, I jumped into the VW and headed up the road.

We had two fixes on the site. The first was based on standing over a spot marked with a football-sized rock—we had hammered nails in the dirt beneath, in case the rock got moved—and sighting over the top of a stick pounded into the side of a berm on the lip of the cliff. The second, not as accurate and some 300 yards to the south, was made by standing on a certain road reflector in the middle of the highway and sighting over the top of a post in the guard rail. When using it we always kept one eye out for traffic.

From the first fix I could see that Ernie and Gary were far off the mark. I found a small piece of white cloth and an old white T-shirt in the VW and began flagging. Since I was still in my black wet suit, the white in my hands should have been plainly visible. The first time, they hit the spot right away. I let out a cheer and waved both hands over my head as Gary dropped anchor. I drove south to the other fix as a double-check.

The second marker indicated they were way off, so I returned to the first one and checked for the nailheads. They weren't there. Had I sent the divers to the wrong spot? Frantically, I groped for the nailheads on all fours, scuffing in the dirt, thinking how efficient our saboteurs had been: first stealing the clips from the lifting bags, then stealing the *Nephripod* and moving the remaining marker-buoy, and now moving the marker-rock.

Suddenly I spied the nailheads. The divers were indeed way off. I got their attention again and went through ten minutes of signalling. I motioned to the right and Gary moved the Speedyak to the right. But when he reached the spot and I waved my hands frantically to indicate that he was on it, he kept going by. I signalled madly to the left, in the meantime cursing and tearing out what was left of my hair because they wouldn't stop. When at last they turned I repeated the whole process in the opposite direction. Again they slid by the mark. Although I could make them out, I thought perhaps they couldn't see me. After 45 minutes of wildly animated signaling, results nil, my arms were tired and throat hoarse.

Just then a woodchopper whom we had named Red Truck Robert pulled up, wanting to know what I was up to. I told him my problem with signaling, suggesting that perhaps what I needed was a larger flag. "I have just the ticket," he said as he dug into the back of his truck, "an old white shirt."

It turned out to be one of the blackest white shirts I had ever seen. I thanked him and continued to signal with what I had.

Another 45 minutes went by, until at last Gary waved the oars. They had found it. The *Nephripod* was still there!

Later, Gary explained that he and Ernie are both blind as bats at a distance without glasses. The only one who saw me at all was Sonny, who was out of shouting range of the others. Sonny said he knew the location by my signals. He could tell exactly where the spot was because every time Gary passed over it Sonny saw me on the cliff going crazy.

Eventually Ernie had found the barrel Jim and I had removed. He came straight up a nearby kelp stalk and then, to mark the position of the barrel, did what he calls "chewing the cabbage off"—chewed the leaves off the top of the bull-kelp bulb, spit them out, and stripped all other foliage off the stalk. The flotation bulb, bare with less weight to support, thrust up high in each trough like a clenched fist, so that it could be seen for quite a distance.

Finally, after following search patterns, he found the *Nephripod*. The marker on the sled had been torn off by storms and the other marker had bounced its anchor along the bottom, away from the site. So there were no pirates after all.

Ernie said he had put a single barrel on the sled. When asked if he tied it down, he said "No." A barrel not tied down would be banged to pieces in short order, but he assured me he hadn't tied it. I still don't understand why he hadn't, except that Ernie did not favor barrels because they were dangerous in the surf.

25. BARRELS AND BREAKERS

I WAS missing Jim now; our group seemed disorganized, and there was no one left to argue with. While it was understood that Ernie was in charge of the lift, he did not like to talk about the things we were going to do—almost as if he were superstitious and pre-planning was bad luck. Perhaps he had developed his methods from years of working alone. He did his planning underwater and was both creative and innovative at it. He got the job done, and sometimes faster and with less fanfare than we did, but his ways and methods were not ours.

The next morning Ernie showed up at nine. We planned only a short dive because of the rough water, to bring the barrels out and tie them on the sled. The rest of the lifting gear could be put on the following day.

We loaded the Avon and Gary and I took the Speedyak out. On my way back to shore Gary whistled to me. The Speedyak was leaking air; he pointed out a small stream of bubbles rising from below the water line. I swam back to him for a conference. We had no patch kit to fix the leak out there, and since the water was getting worse, we decided to cancel our plans for the day.

We shed our wet suits on the beach. By this time the sun was out, and we lay high on the warm sand talking over our individual plans for the afternoon. Ernie was thinking of going to the Cove to look for jade. Since the water was calming I thought I might dive in the surf or just sunbathe and Sonny and Gary decided to body surf.

Then an unusual thing happened. While we were talking the water calmed completely. It now looked as if we were on a tropical beach— the sun on the sand, the blue transparent water, and tiny waves delicately lapping the shore. We were hypnotized by the sudden change, and it was a while before we realized that since it was so calm and the Avon was already loaded it would be an ideal time to put the barrels on the sled.

We suited up again and Ernie and I rode the Avon out. Sonny and Gary were going to bring the barrels to us through the surf, Sonny swimming them out.

As soon as Ernie and I got the Avon out beyond the breaker line the wind came up again with twice the force it had had before. The sea began to get rough; all at once became exceedingly nasty. Back toward shore we could see Sonny beyond the huge breakers, trying to bring the barrels through while Gary helped him from shore. They were in trouble.

Ernie explained that the proper way to bring the barrels through the surf was to be in the trough when the barrel was on the crest of a wave, because if both you and the barrel were hit by sets of incoming waves at the same time both you and the barrel would be washed to shore. If you were in the trough when the barrel was hit on the crest you could muscle the barrel over the wave. I decided that Ernie should go back and show Sonny how to get them through.

Even with Ernie's help they couldn't be brought out. One barrel flipped high into the air, and I saw Gary take it up on the beach. Finally I saw that all the barrels were on the sand. The barrels had been pounded severely. Many of them were dented and their hoops were bent and their hooks broken. It would take a lot of work to make them useful again.

Meanwhile, the ocean beyond me had roughened to hurricane proportions. The sky was darkening and the wind whipped stinging spray-like sleet across the tops of waves. I picked my way through the waves, taking the Avon in large circles, going out about twice as far as I normally would have, then back in as close to the breaker line as I dared, the spray burning my eyes. What worried me most was that the motor was running out of gas, and I knew it would be impossible for me to refill. I was sure that when it gave its final dry cough I would be blown into the huge breakers, where I would be in real trouble and might lose much expensive equipment.

At last a signal from shore sent me immediately toward the point, where the waves looked smaller. Once there I steered in small ovals beyond the breakers, waiting for the others, who were slowly walking up the beach. When they got close I waited for a swell to pass, then gunned the motor. A swell rose under the Avon, then became a boiling wave that drove the raft forward. It picked up speed, shooting me shoreward. I shouted "Yaa-hoo!" as the churning wave rocketed me in like a surfboard: Makaha Charlie, on the big one! It looked as if it would set me high up on the beach.

I shouted to the others to hold the raft from the backwash so I could make a high and dry landing. They ran to help, and as I reached back to shut off the motor and tilt it up so the propeller wouldn't drag against the gravel I saw that the raft had been riding a double wave. The second and larger one was trailing close behind me. It caught up, rose high above me, and dumped itself into the raft, knocking me into the water. I knew the raft would swing over me in the backwash, so I dove for the bottom and waited for the blow, my hands over my head for protection. Fortunately, it didn't hit me. I finally came up and we got the gear ashore.

We had had enough of rough seas for one day. We decided that rather than haul our gear back to camp we would leave it on the beach overnight. There were ten tanks, the diving equipment, the Speedyak, the Avon, the two motors, and other gear. That night we staggered our eating and sleeping schedules so that someone was always on guard.

The next day the ocean was still rough, so we decided to postpone our salvage efforts for a while. We decided to move all our equipment off the beach before breakfast. Carrying the equipment down the long sandy beach, across a stretch of rocks, through the creek and up a short incline to the vehicles represented hours of heavy work—especially hauling the dented barrels, one by one, on our shoulders. We weren't finished until noon. Then Gary fixed us a belated breakfast, treating us to a gourmet special: steaks marinated in Japanese wine!

Back home in San Francisco I found the hole in the side of the Speedyak and repaired it, along with other holes in the bottom. I checked the Avon over, but being a heavier, much better built craft for the type of work we were doing, it had no punctures.

I visited Jim in the hospital. He was loafing around like a king and getting fat while waiting for his eye operation. I tried to reassure him, not too convincingly, that things were working out just fine and that we were on the verge of popping the *Nephripod* out of the sea.

26. SUCCESS

ON JUNE 8 I returned to the Cove and dove with Sonny. Gary was due the next morning, but the water was so calm I telephoned him to leave immediately. Then I called Ernie, who promised to be there early the next morning with four large float bags.

The barrels were in such bad shape that we couldn't use them. Even with Ernie's float bags our lift would be marginal. Ernie's bags were completely closed, not opened on the bottom like the small lifting bags. They had no exhaust valves to release air under increased pressure, so we didn't dare fill them to capacity on the sea floor, since the volume of air would increase about four times on their way up. This meant that at a depth of 70 feet only one-fourth of the bag's total capacity could be put to use. At that depth each one would lift only 1,250 pounds and the four of them only 5,000 pounds, so to start the rock on its way up we would still have to raise 4,000 pounds with our remaining lift bags. If we were lucky enough to get the rock started, though, the expanding air on the way up would provide more than adequate buoyancy. Two of the large float bags would support 10,000 pounds at the surface, and we had four of them.

The next day dawned on a calm sea. We took a quick drive to Willow Creek and found that the water there looked like a mill pond. I had never seen it so calm. Excitement mounted in me like an immense tide.

Although we had planned to leave Jade Cove, we switched our launching point to Willow Creek. We took the Speedyak to tow the jade and once again loaded gear into the Avon. We not only had the extra float bags but also eight tanks for filling the bags, three tanks apiece for diving, and the remaining lifting bags. Behind us we pulled Ernie's tire tube with three air tanks in it. At the last moment Sonny threw in five truck tire tubes "just in case we need some extra flotation."

The water remained calm as we reached the site. We anchored on the buoy and swam down with two of Ernie's large float bags. Ernie and Sonny began to tie them on while I secured the tow rope to the sled.

When I went to help with the bags one of them got twisted so that the valve was high. This posed a problem when we pumped air into it, since if a valve is high air leaks out once the fill tank is pulled away, and before the float can be capped water can get in. By this time Ernie's four float bags were below, and Ernie was tying on the last two. Then Sonny and I began to put on the lifting bags, first clipping on as many as we could and then trying to find them to fill them instead of filling each as it was attached. This was a mistake, because the empty bags got stuck behind the full ones and were easily missed. This, plus the fact that the old bags were still there, compounded the confusion. The old bags, now in the water almost a month, were so tattered and torn that they would not hold air.

When the lifting bags were all on I started filling a large float bag. I was low on air, and as I went to replace the valve I dropped it under the sled. I squeezed beneath the sled as far as I could get, but the valve was five to six inches beyond my fingertips. When I started backing out my diving tank hung up on some rope. I couldn't reach back to untangle the tank or cut the rope. I was helpless.

I didn't have enough air to engage in a long, possibly futile struggle to free myself, so I needed help fast. I looked for Sonny but saw that he had gone up to change tanks. Then I saw Ernie working on the other side of the sled.

Swinging my body violently, I thrust my tank three times against the metal sled above me, "clank, clank, clank...."

Ernie kept on working. I banged the tank on the sled three times again and waited. Nothing happened. Three more times. Ernie, concentrating, made no response.

I knew then that I would have to get out by myself. I undid the tank straps and slipped the tank off. Once it was off and untangled I could hold it so that it would not bind, and then I could reach the valve. With regulator still in my mouth I held the tank away from the sled in one hand, and by scooting my body under the sled I was just able to grab the valve. I palmed it, slid out, and quickly put the valve on the float bag. Then I swam for the surface, my tank in my arms, sucking it dry as I rose through the water.

After I had rested for a while, Gary helped me on with another tank and I went down to help Ernie finish filling the lifting bags. Then I joined Sonny in tying on and filling tire tubes. Since I had been filling bags from my regulator rather than with one of the separate fill tanks, I was low on air again. Finally we had filled all the flotation bags, as well as the tire tubes.

There was a slight surge even at that depth, and the rock, beginning to shift with it, looked as though it was ready to go. To see if it would rise

I planted my feet firmly on the sea floor, straining upward on the lowest corner of the sled. The corner rose easily, but to my horror another corner sank down and the whole sled suddenly shifted with a jerk to an almost vertical position, so that the light end was now almost directly above the heavy end. When this happened the air in the bags on the now higher end must have expanded slightly, making the load even more unbalanced. The sudden shift was frightening, and since many of the chains which bound the rock to the sled were now broken I was afraid the Nephripod would slide off the sled. If the rock slid off, the sled with all the lifting gear would rocket to the surface, possibly taking the divers with it.

I ran out of air and swam to the surface. Since only a little more inflating was necessary I was sure that the rock would rise before I could put on a fresh tank, so I climbed aboard with Gary and we paddled the Avon with the Speedyak tied behind it to a respectable distance from the buoy.

Suddenly the surface of the water was broken by myriads of bubbles, and the sea began to churn as if it were going to erupt. There was a huge splash as a massive amount of air burst to the surface, and a long, awesome hiss. Then the water rose up like a liquid mountain. I held my breath. All at once Ernie's huge black bags belched out of the depths and the Nephripod was on the surface! It was like a small island that rocked back and forth, seeking its own level, accompanied by the hissing of bubbles and escaping air.

The bags rode much higher than I had thought they would. We thought that one of the large bags might be broken, but none were, even though one of them was so over-inflated it was jutting out through the rope net in a waffle-like pattern. The tire tubes bulged like great, lopsided doughnuts. Even if they had exploded on the way up the expansion of air in the other floats would have contributed enough lift power to have brought the rock the rest of the way up. Now that the Nephripod was on the surface there was a tremendous safety margin.

I jumped into the water and helped deflate some of the float bags, to keep them from expanding further in the heat of the sun and to try to balance the load, which was listing heavily. We found several unfilled lifting bags we had missed, moved them to the low side and blew air into them. All in all, the sled was only four feet below the surface, shallow enough so it would ride in high on the beach.

The sea remained calm, even though a slight breeze had sprung up. Ernie and I climbed into the Avon and the others got into the Speedyak to tow the rock.

Although we had a heavy load of tanks in the Avon we landed easily, riding in on a small wave. The surf was so calm that one diver held the raft in position while the other took the gear high up on the beach. Then we turned the Avon upside down over the gear and walked to the south end of the beach.

Ernie had definite ideas on where the rock should come in and on what the reef situation was below the water, so he directed the landing. Gary and Sonny, who had been holding the rock offshore while we unloaded the Avon, moved in closer while I swam out to them with a long yellow nylon line, one end of which was attached to an anchored snatch block on shore. Sonny tied the tow rope from the Speedyak to the nylon line.

The surf was so calm that one diver had no problem pushing the *Nephipod* by himself, bringing it in exactly where Ernie directed. As we brought it in I looked down through the water and saw that the sled was clearing the rocky reef by a good two feet. We brought it up on the sand as far as we could with a slight boost from the small breakers. The rock landed fairly high and dry and, helped by the rising tide and the grip-hoist, we pulled it up farther.

When the tide rose it covered the *Nephripod*, but it was safe.

Late that afternoon we all went to the Pacific Valley store to celebrate.

I telephoned Jim at the hospital.

"James?"

"Hi, Don, how's it going?"

"The *Nephripod* is on the beach! It came in beautifully!"

"Thank God!"

I told Jim how it had gone and what a great job Ernie had done.

Jim was elated. He was getting out of the hospital in a day or so and wanted to come down to help get the rock up the beach and onto the trailer.

We had a big dinner with champagne. Ernie, his job completed, went home, an extra day's pay in his pocket as a bonus.

27. ON THE BEACH

DURING THE NIGHT I was restless. The sounds of the sea were steady, a ceaseless roar that rose and fell, almost dying and then coming alive again. Immense swells were lifting far out to sea, pulled toward the coast by invisible forces, following one another forever in a vast cosmic timetable.

Gary and Sonny went back to the house trailer at the campground and I slept in my VW at Willow Creek.

There were two tide cycles a day; the Nephripod had been floated in on the low-high tide, but now the high-high tide covered it. I thought of the Nephripod being scoured by the sand and undermined by the tide, once again, for a while, claimed by the sea. Lying on its steel pyre it was like some great dead bird washed in by the waves, its breast raised to the moon.

I got up to relieve myself. To the south I could see the black, jagged profile of Cape San Martin, its red beacon blinking against the sky. The ocean had gotten rougher. How lucky we had been to have had such a calm day to bring the Nephripod in, I thought. The sea rocked in the bowl of Willow Cove. The shadows of waves advanced like black sails. The white flesh of a wave broke the darkness suddenly, erupted into the moonlight, then quickly dissolved.

Perhaps fulfillment lies in being lost in moonlight, I thought, in the sun and in the sea, in the endless stream of life—in being, and not in thinking about being.

Later, back in the VW I was swept through a narrow tunnel of jade in the darkness of a dream. I could see its swirling white and green pattern, as if its whole surface were flowing with incredible light. Carried down through the tunnel by an unending current of foam, I could touch the jade but couldn't gain a handhold. My fingernails scratched on smooth, impenetrable surfaces as I was sucked into sudden darkness.

I woke early and dressed quickly. The tide was out. Through the half-light I made out the Nephripod, once again exposed to the air. When I got to the rock I saw that it had been half buried by the tide, so I dug down through the damp sand until I could feel the cold steel of the sled.

I jumped into the VW and drove to the campground. The others were still sleeping. Not wanting to be delayed by waking them and waiting until they got dressed—because I was afraid someone might come along the beach and take a chunk out of our rock—I grabbed a shovel and some boards and went back to Willow Creek.

After digging a hole to expose the sled I went back and roused the sleeping beauties, explaining that we had better get to work fast because the tide was on its way in.

Back at Willow Creek the three of us wedged boards under the sled and attached the small griphoist, then wrapped the cable around several large rocks. When we pumped on the griphoist the sled barely budged. It seemed to be hung up. One of the shingled metal plates on the bottom had sprung, probably when the sled had sunk and dropped on the rocks in 70 feet of water.

It took two men to work the griphoist. As we strained to pull the sled out of the hole something suddenly gave. The cable, the high-tensile-strength chain, the shackles, and one of the loops of steel Jim had welded to the sled had broken. When we looked we saw that one of the metal plates was folded completely back.

Tarkin arrived with his wife and daughter. The little girl climbed on top of the rock. From the highest part, looking down, flowing green shapes could be seen all around—like being on an island of jade! Tarkin looked the rock over thoroughly, caressing its surface sensually with his long fingers.

I said, "This rock, it's taken me 15 years to pick up this rock."

He and his family then strolled south down the beach, heads bowed, searching the gravel. The mist coming off the waves in the morning wind suspended itself around them, creating an ethereal atmosphere. Above that, dark draws deep with sinew and strength led to the summits of purple ridge upon ridge, the sun flanking their brows with gold, and a light blue sky beyond

We switched to the large griphoist, but it soon jammed as if it were broken. We finally had to quit. We had dragged the *Nephripod* only 35 feet.

At about noon the tide washed over the rock, so we went to Pacific Valley store for beer and to call Jim. He told us that he was getting out of the hospital the next day. The operation had been unsuccessful, however, and his eye was no better. He suggested that we take the griphoist apart so that if it needed parts he could bring them with him when he came down.

We disassembled the griphoist, cleaned out all the sand and gravel, greased it, and reassembled it. It worked fine. Sonny came up with the

Sonny pulls the *Nephripod* with the griphoist, Cape San Martin in the background.

The *Seagull* outboard, barrels, and other gear strewn around the trailer.

idea of extending the griphoist handle with a long pipe so that one man could work it by walking the handle back and forth while the others kept the sled from binding. But we couldn't get the pipes straight under the sled, and we had too few pipes and timbers and were short on cable. Also, because of a combination of irregular meals, exhaustion, and psychological letdown, we were done in by noon, our energy drained. We had moved the rock only 40 feet.

It was a blessing that the afternoon high tide submerged the rock so that we didn't have to worry about it being chipped by rock hounds. We drove back to camp and quietly dissolved for the afternoon. The weather was warm, so after mending our broken equipment we hauled our sleeping bags onto the grass around the house trailer to doze and relax.

By this time we had attracted a following of old people who wanted to hear about our adventure. One old fellow told us that we could move the rock easier by building an "A" frame over it, slinging the rock in between, and inching it up the beach, "the way the Egyptians did it." An old couple usually three sheets to the wind by mid-afternoon, showed up daily, cocktails in hand, expecting entertainment, until finally they would tire of us and wander off.

This particular afternoon I lay on my sleeping bag listening to the plaintive song of a bird in a nearby tree, while another of the same species answered him, proclaiming territorial rights. They kept up their chatter for a long time, back and forth, until I drifted off to sleep.

A sharp rock poking me in the back annoyed me into a state of semiconsciousness. I rolled over, opening one eye a slit to check the height of the sun. That was a mistake.

A voice crackled, "Hi, young feller, I see you're awake."

I opened both eyes. It was one of the old buzzards sitting nearby on a camp bench, waiting for some indication of life. I groaned inwardly, but he had already begun to chatter. My rest was ruined.

Finally, Jim showed up on Saturday with a friend from Clear Lake, Johnny Ingram. General Custer would not have been so relieved to see reinforcements as was I to see James and company. They arrived in a large flatbed truck with some big boards and plenty of chain, cable, metal pipe, and other goodies. They continued on south to get more supplies and to pick up the jade trailer that was stored at Sonny's sister's at Cambria.

Gary, Sonny, and I spent yet another morning dragging the rock up the beach, again working until the tide came in. We jockeyed the rock into position in back of a gigantic rock that rose about 20 feet out of the sand, feeling that the *Nephripod* would be secure from the tide there.

Ernie dropped by and helped us move rocks to make a road so our vehicles could get close to the beach. He had a big sledge hammer and attacked the rocks with it like one possessed. He seemed to enjoy beating on rock; perhaps this was the key to his nature—his "man against mountain" syndrome.

Jim and his friend Johnny Ingram returned at night. Jim eased some large steaks from a grocery bag. Our mouths watered as he unwrapped them and we saw how big and thick each one was, with abundant red juices running from them. We looked longingly at them as they were dumped along with carrots, potatoes, tomatoes, and onions into that great equalizer to be heated until the whistle blew.

We had missed Jim, and as we sat around the table eating steaks by candlelight he announced that he intended to have the rock on the jade trailer by the following night, since Johnny had to be home. We didn't think it was possible.

I brought up a subject which had been bothering Sonny, Gary, and me for the last three days, something we hadn't thought much about until the rock was out of the water. Most people who saw the rock brought up the same subject. Some took longer than others, but inevitably they would lead up to it. It had to do with values:

"Uh, what do you think it's worth?"

"What do you mean?"

"I mean, how much can you get for it? How much money?"

Always the same question. They couldn't understand why we would have brought the *Nephripod* up if we weren't going to sell it. We couldn't tell them that we had brought up the *Nephripod* just to see if we could do it, or for fun, for companionship, to give us an excuse to drink beer, or because we found it to be a meaningful symbol. We couldn't tell them that we did it because we like the feel of jade and wanted other people to share our love of jade with us. They wouldn't understand we did it because it was a challenge, because of some deep need within us—or because we found ourselves committed to a task without any logical reason at all.

People couldn't understand that. Yet they marry for love, go to church for a promise, climb mountains "because they are there," explore because of curiosity, go to war for honor, fear, the flag, and a host of other reasons. And lots of them devote their "unproductive" time to hobbies that have no monetary rewards at all.

For three days we told people, "Go look at it and feel it. It's worth whatever you get out of it."

But this didn't satisfy them. They would return and say, "Seriously, what do you *really* think it's worth?"

But Gary and Sonny and I didn't know what it was worth.

As we sat around the table in the trailer that night we put the question to Jim, the master rockhound of the group. Jim had been considering its value while he was in the hospital, looking up records of other finds and reading back copies of the *Lapidary Journal* and other magazines.

"Well, good Monterey jade should go for a minimum of $20 a pound. And the *Nephripod* is as good a piece of Monterey jade as I've ever seen. If it weighs 8,000 pounds that should make it worth $160,000."

Gary, Sonny, and I were flabbergasted. We couldn't tell people it was worth that much, so for a few weeks, when anyone asked us what the *Nephripod* was worth we pointed to Jim and said, "Ask him." And Jim told them. (After a while, though, we got so we could say it easily.)

The following morning as we were driving from the campground we saw the *Nephripod* on Willow Creek beach from about a mile away. It was a landmark! Amazing! That huge rock was ours, and it was all jade!

We had a full crew again, plus some extra hands to boot. Although Jim's doctor had warned him not to work (he had to wear dark glasses which made him look like a Greek shipping tycoon), we were right in suspecting that he would do a lot more than soil his hands. Jim's friend Johnny Ingram also pitched in. The funny baseball hat perched on top of his head and the perpetual smile on his face were deceptive. I have never seen anyone work so hard. He didn't even stop for lunch but, with a sandwich in one hand and a crowbar in the other, he just kept on working. Other helpers came too. Ernie showed up in his Sunday duds, which didn't deter him from putting in many hours of hard work. Two friends of Ernie's, Don Pemberton and Lonnie Price, owner of a rock shop in Cambria, also came to help. Sonny, Gary, and I had suddenly become the dispossessed, and we gladly let the new workers take over.

Since it was Sunday a flock of tourists had descended upon us. Not recognizing the *Nephripod* to be jade, they asked what all the excitement was about and why we were working on the rock. At first we tried to explain; but it took too much time, and they still didn't understand. So we tried to tell them a story they could accept, that we had found this beautiful rock that my wife was crazy about pretty rocks and that I was going to take it home for our rock garden. That satisfied most of them.

We dug the sled out of the sand again, then brought four 25 foot long 4 x 10 beams, which Jim had somehow acquired from the old Ghirardelli Chocolate Building in San Francisco, down to the beach.

We moved rocks and put the wooden beams on top of them to form a ramp up to the bed of the jade trailer. We hooked the griphoist to the Bronco, which was in front of the jade trailer, and braced the wheels with rocks. The weight of the *Nephripod* almost dragged the Bronco and jade trailer down onto the beach. Then we strung cable from the Bronco to the flatbed truck. Sonny, Gary, and I pumped on the large griphoist, using the small one to take up the slack so that if the large one slipped the sled would still be under control.

The executive committee, Jim, Johnny, Ernie, and Don, held many conferences involving many theoretical arguments about procedures and other complex things that we wanted no part of. Every time the executives talked theory, Sonny, Gary, and I placed our bottoms securely on some likely looking boulder. Finally, late that afternoon, the sled with the huge rock chained to it was rolled up the incline and onto the jade trailer.

We removed the griphoists and other gear. Then we drove the truck up the hill onto the road above, where it could get a good purchase. A long cable was strung between the Bronco and the flatbed truck. With both vehicles pulling, and with me photographing the action, the trailer lurched forward about ten feet on the sand and rock incline we had built. Then the Bronco lost traction and dug itself to a halt, its tires spinning as a cloud of dust rose around it.

Somehow our signals got crossed. Jim was rocking the Bronco back and forth to get its wheels out of the holes they had dug, while at the same time the truck up above jerked forward. The strain on the jade trailer sheared off the ball and socket which bound it to the Bronco, and the jade trailer with the *Nephripod* on top of it was suddenly free and rolling back toward the sea!

I was so surprised that I stopped filming—the sign of an amateur photographer. Ernie, reacting instantly, grabbed a rock and ran to throw it behind the wheel of the jade trailer. Fortunately, the trailer ran into another rock and stopped of its own accord.

We backed up the Bronco and put a new hitch on. This time we pulled the jade trailer all the way out and onto the pavement. Then we removed all the cables, and the Bronco pulled the *Nephripod* up the Willow Creek grade without any trouble.

Jim (right) and Don Pemberton build a wooden ramp up to the trailer bed.

We move the huge rock toward the trailer just ahead of the incoming afternoon tide (left to right: Johnny Ingram, Don Pemberton, Sonny).

Tourists are fascinated by our project (far left, Johnny Ingram; far right, Sonny).

At last, the 9,000-pound gemstone rests on the trailer.

At 6:00 p.m., in caravan, we headed to Pacific Valley. We left our rock outside while we had dinner on Jim and me, complete with champagne.

The *Nephripod* remained in front of the store all night. Sonny slept in his truck nearby, his trusty gun by his side.

28. A NATIONAL MONUMENT

THE NEXT MORNING I took over the *Nephripod* watch, polishing the huge stone with a rag and talking to curious passers-by, including a busload of tourists.

We got on the road about eleven, Jim driving the Bronco towing the *Nephripod* and Johnny and I following in the truck. We were tailing Jim in case he had trouble, but we had also planned to pass him at specific places so I could film. We shot movies as the Bronco crossed Limekiln Creek bridge and again a few miles farther north as Jim drove by at a 30-mph clip.

Just south of Big Sur State Park we came to a long, steep downhill grade. Suddenly we heard a siren and saw a flashing red light coming up the grade toward us. We slowed down, our hearts in our throats. The oncoming car slowed, winking its bright red light at Jim. Johnny geared down, and above the sound of the truck motor we heard an amplified voice say, "Pull over!"

Jim started braking the trailer, ever so slowly. The electric brakes had been adjusted poorly, and every time Jim touched them they locked on the trailer, skidding the Bronco to an abrupt halt—not the best way to stop a rig carrying that much weight.

I said to Johnny, "Where in hell is he going to pull off? It looks like we've had it!"

Just then Jim came to a wide graveled area on the righthand side of the road and he swung onto it, the wheels of the trailer grabbing gravel and skidding. Jim brought the whole rig to a magnificent halt in a swirl of dust.

The sheriff, who had had to make a U-turn hadn't seen that Jim had had trouble stopping. As we pulled up behind the *Nephripod* the sheriff's car slid around both of us and parked in front of the Bronco.

The sheriff and Jim jumped out of their respective vehicles simultaneously. Jim told me later that he was worried about every violation in the vehicle code book: the trailer, the brake lights, the turn signals, the hitch, the weight of the load he was hauling, and more. The sheriff was a big bruiser. "What-cha-got there?"

"Well, er, it's a jade rock."

"Well, we have a complaint that you are making off with a national monument."

"A national monument? Well I ... no, it's from the sea; we got it underwater. We're scuba divers."

"Where did you get it?"

"Well, sir, from Jade Cove. It's not a national monument. It's easy to tell it came from the sea."

By this time encrustations on the huge stone were beginning to rot— tunicates, sea anemones, rock scallops, bryozoa, coralline algae. An old piece of kelp hung down like a piece of surgical tubing.

Johnny and I confirmed that it was from the sea. "Look at all those dead animals."

Certainly he could smell and see that this was no ordinary national monument. He walked around the trailer and put his hand on the rock and smelled his fingers. Then he inspected the lights, braking system, safety chains.

"Jade Cove, huh? How much does it weigh?"

Jim polished his halo, "We haven't weighed it yet."

"Well, I'd say around three or four thousand pounds." He motioned to Jim. "Come over to my car."

Johnny whispered to me, "Three or four thousand! He must be thinking of lava rock."

Jim was walking around with the sheriff, explaining as he went how we had floated the *Nephripod*.

I said to Johnny, "I should be getting this on film. I wonder if he would mind."

The sheriff went back to his car and took a large manual out of his glove compartment. He searched through it for a while.

"Well, I can't see any way you've broken the law...."

Then I timidly inquired, "Officer, we're making a movie of this rock; you know, how we got it underwater and so on. Would you mind if we shot some pictures of this? This would be great in the film, Jim getting arrested and all...."

He attempted to smile. "I guess it would be O.K. But I'll have to check in with headquarters to find out the exact nature of the complaint against you."

The sheriff had his car door open and was standing half in and half out of it, making radio contact with his office. I ran to the truck, grabbed the camera, and ran back. Jim was standing beside the sheriff awkwardly, with one hand in his pocket.

"Hey, Jim, don't look at the camera."

Jim shrugged his shoulders as I began to shoot. The sheriff got out of his car and Jim made fists and held both arms out to him subserviently, his wrists held together as if he were going to be handcuffed. He looked over at the camera to see if I was shooting, then remembered what I had told him, shrugged his shoulders again and looked up into the trees.

The sheriff said, "It seems some lady saw you drive by and issued a complaint. She said she thought you were stealing a national monument. But headquarters says no national monuments are missing. I'm sorry, but I still have to fill out a report. Then I'll let you go."

We had decided to take the *Nephripod* to Jim's cabin at Clear Lake, where we would have space to clean and polish it. After our encounter with the sheriff, though, we decided to leave it at my uncle's house for a while so Jim could work over the braking system and we could shift the load so that it would ride better.

My aunt Lyle is an avid collector of oriental jade. She, of course, was delighted to see us, and since it was her birthday she naturally assumed that we had brought her a mammoth present. She invited all the neighbors over to see the rock.

One morning as she was scraping dishes and she looked out the kitchen window to see her Japanese gardener circling around the rock. She went out to see what he was doing.

He speaks little English, but she overheard him muttering over and over, "Gee-sus Crice, Gee-sus Crice!" He told her later that he prospects for California jade himself, up at Happy Camp in the Sierra.

Within a week, Jim and I climbed into the Bronco and, with the jade in tow again, headed for Clear Lake. On the way we pulled in at an official State Weighing station. When we deducted the weight of the trailer we found that the *Nephripod* actually weighed 9,000 pounds! We had gained $20,000 in ten minutes!

At Jim's place we parked the trailer out back under a large oak tree, in a spot where the *Nephripod* could be worked on.

While the rock was still in the sea one of my fantasies had been, if we ever got it out, to clean it up and tow it through Chinatown, San Francisco. I thought the Chinese would go wild when they saw such a beautiful, large chunk of jade. Jim disagreed, claiming that Chinese are unemotional, and would probably ignore it, the debate usually ending with me insisting we take it to Chinatown anyway, "just for fun." I wanted to film whatever the reaction, good or bad. Also, there was a San Francisco Gem and Mineral Show, put on by Jim's rock hound club, where Jim was anxious to show. We would do both.

29. JADE IS A WOMAN

THERE WAS NOT the slightest doubt that Jim lived in more civilized surroundings than either Gary or I. Even his country cabin, perched on a bluff at Clear Lake, could be considered elegant, at the very least. The cabin had grown into a house through his own handiwork with a room added here and another room there. Its most prominent feature was a large living room with a formidable rock fireplace and a glass wall revealing a view of the entire lake. The cabin was sprinkled with antiques, among which were a player piano, a white Chinese Buddha, a large coral-colored coffee grinder made into a lamp, a spinning wheel, and a three-foot-high wooden brown bear raised up on its hind legs and shackled through the collar by a long wooden chain. Museum-quality mineral specimens from all over the world were on the floor, on tables, and in special cabinets. Under the living room was a combination garage and machine shop.

Outside was a sprawling rock garden which looked like a public park, and jade and other rocks were strewn randomly around, the Green Pickle among them. Over the entrance to the garden hung a broken and weather-worn sign Jim had found washed up and abandoned at Willow Creek; it read JADE COVE. Between the rock garden and the cabin, under a large oak tree, we parked the jade trailer with the Nephripod on it.

Jim, Gary, and I spent almost a week scraping down the rock and cleaning it. We used wire brushes, buffers, scrapers, carborundum discs, sandblasting equipment, and anything else we could get our hands on.

Jim's cabin is located in an area of retirement homes and elderly people from the neighborhood often dropped by to spin yarns with him. Jim was always nice to them, lending tools, fabricating things for them,

Gary wears a mask while sandblasting encrustations off the *Nephripod*.

I "work over" the *Nephripod* with an electric grinder.

and, best of all, serving coffee and cookies. They usually came by from eight to ten in the morning and from six to eight in the evening. At these times the yard was a center of activity—one of the main attractions of Lake County. As they were being served they sat on the wooden deck and watched us at our task.

During that hot and dusty week we used nitric acid on the *Nephripod* to boil off coralline algae and other stubborn encrustations. We also used a sandblaster and carborundum wheels, which blanketed the rock, the oak tree and us with white dust and showered us with flying sparks. Toward the end of the week the *Nephripod* began to look good. Swirled surfaces, obscured until then, glowed with a new radiance and felt sleek beneath our hands as we polished them.

On an especially hot day Jim went to San Francisco for a doctor's appointment, leaving Gary and me to finish work on the rock.

Gary and I were O.K. We had enough food, lots of materials for our work, and a couple of six-packs in the refrigerator to slake our thirst.

By noon we had only consumed one beer apiece. And that was pretty good, seeing that the dust off the rock settled everywhere and our throats were particularly parched. We took our noon break in Captain's chairs, sitting in the shade on the deck consuming two tuna and pickle sandwiches and a couple of beers and surveying our land and the rock that rested on it. After lunch the day grew hotter and stickier and the sun climbed to a point where the oak tree no longer offered shade over the rock.

By late afternoon, after time out for a swim, a nap, and several beers, we were almost done. Gary suggested that we wash the rock down to see how it would look, so we lovingly hosed the *Nephripod*— and ourselves too. The rock looked beautiful, fantastic! The sun's rays, slanting now, seemed to give it an ethereal quality. I took a small piece of sandpaper and delicately went over one spot that still had a bit of coralline on it, then polished it with a rag. As I rubbed the rock I began to feel a sort of sensual pleasure. Not sexual, but sensual, as one might get pleasure from listening to certain kinds of music.

It occurred to me that our sense of touch was very primitive—certainly more primitive, in an evolutionary sense, than our faculties of hearing, or seeing, and it also occurred to me that the sense of touch is something we can easily tune in to, or fall back on. We miss it in sculpture and painting; there aren't enough things in our museums that people can appreciate esthetically through touch. The *Nephripod* was not only beautiful to see but beautiful to touch.

Gary was also polishing the rock.

"Hey," he said, "this rock feels sexy. I mean, it really feels *sexy!*"

We stopped working to think about that, and to cool ourselves while we were thinking I went up to the house for the last of the beer. As we were talking about how the rock felt to us I explained my museum idea to Gary.

"Hey, I got an idea!" Gary said. "Why not write a letter to *Playboy Magazine* about the rock?"

Suddenly ideas were coming so fast and furious that we decided to go up to the cabin for a pencil and paper. To get in the mood, and because the sun had set, we had a few philosophical drinks. We got in the mood all right, but we needed a copy of *Playboy* to see what style the letter should take, so we drove to the store and bought a *Playboy* and a bottle of cold duck. Once back at the cabin we sat between the white Buddha and the three-foot-high wooden brown bear and composed this letter:

Dear Hugh (Hefner):

Enclosed are pictures of a nine thousand pound piece of jade which we discovered and salvaged from off the Big Sur coast in California. This rock is the largest pure nodule of nephrite jade in the United States, possibly the world.

Because of the diverse nature of your magazine we think this gem has definite pictorial possibilities which would interest your readers.

There is a great re-emergence these days in touch stones, worry stones, or security stones (depending upon your psychic needs); and jade is popular in this because of the ancient oriental tradition which gives this stone a particular symbolic aura (who knows what they actually did with their stones?).

This to us would lend itself to interesting photographic prospects, i.e., body rubbing (parties?).

All sorts of possibilities spring into one's (male) mind: What do you say (do) to a naked lady? What does a naked lady do with a nine thousand pound piece of jade?

I recall seeing your display of girls of France, Sweden, etc. On this rock you could display girls of the Orient, for what is more oriental than jade?

Or, since this piece of jade came from the sea off the coast of Big Sur, it would lend itself beautifully to a pictorial display of the people of Big Sur.

Big Sur. Rock = symbol or origin of Big Sur country.

Everyone that comes near the rock rubs it. You can't approach it without caressing and feeling it (feeling of a woman implied here).

Where could a girl be displayed more beautifully?

Feeling of a woman and the feeling of jade are so synonymous, one enhances the other.

Scene: Japanese tea garden. Jasmine or lotus blossoms over the jade. Two Japanese girls having tea? Are they dressed?

Art Excerpt: Jade carved by the sea: Chinese art. One is created by Nature, the other by man. Both indicate simplicity, beauty, and tranquility.

First rubbing the hands on the jade, then for the more free, the bodies. Jade seems to carry us back to our very beginnings, to the oneness of Nature. Free yourself!

What could be more basic than the sea or the feeling of a rock? Both draw you back to primitive origins: jade has this quality more than any other rock.

Green is a creative symbol (you know, plants, and all that).

Jade, contoured by the sea and the elements. The sea symbolizes eternity. Jade: life and creativity.

Pictures:

1. Very feminine, delicate hand with jade ring on it. Sexy arrangement of hand on rock.
2. Luscious girl with jewelry on, body blending with lines of rock.
3. Sea and the jade.
4. Flowing of jade and flowing lines of girl's body and flowing lines of the sea.
5. Profile of prone girl's body and jade with no indication of where body begins or jade ends (except for pastel colors, warm skin tones, cool green jade); has effect on man like snake in Garden of Eden—green snake and warm woman—something coming between man and his woman.
6. Woman caressing rock with her body.
7. Woman leaning backward over jade. All sorts of possibilities, OR just face and hair in picture, hair curled down jade like waterfall.

Why would a guy trade his empire for a piece of jade he has never seen?

Where else could the gem be displayed with the beauty of its color and the contour of its shape, which is so synonymous to the beauty of a woman?

Fashion Display: Jade jewelry, earrings, necklace, nothing else on model.

Jade is a woman.

It was stiflingly hot in the house, so we decided to go outside. But we changed our minds when we saw a congregation of senior citizens clustered around the *Nephripod*. We quietly closed the door, shut off the kitchen light, and scurried back to the security of the living room. We didn't want to be seen by the senior citizens in our present carefree condition; and besides, we were having fun being creative, which we thought they wouldn't understand.

There was a knock on the door. There was no way we could get away and hide. I felt like I had been caught with my hand in the cookie jar.

But it was only Johnny Ingram and his wife. What a relief! We told them about our idea for *Playboy Magazine* and how it had evolved.

After the Ingrams left we decided that Hugh Hefner would not be able to visualize our highly imaginative photographic essay properly, so we decided that somehow we would have to supply him with photographs. Gary volunteered to find a photographer. As a matter of fact, he *did* know a beautiful woman photographer who not only took pictures but was also a model herself. She knew some other models too, so Gary decided it would be up to him to maintain control and do all the interviewing personally.

Just as there are day people and night people, there are also day ideas and night ideas. At any rate, in the clearer light of the next day I couldn't find much to say in support of the *Playboy* caper. And when I mentioned it to Jim a week later he just stared at me.

30. A STATE OF MIND

WE TOOK the cleaned and polished *Nephripod* to San Francisco to be within striking distance of Chinatown and the San Francisco Gem and Mineral Show.

The rock was too wide to fit in an ordinary garage, so unless we could find a home for it, it had to be left out on the street. I explained the situation to an old friend, Dustin Chivers, of the California Academy of Sciences, to see if the Academy might have a place for it. They didn't, but Dusty, never at a loss for ideas, found a spot. An employee of the Academy, Paul Deignon, was taking care of a mansion out in the Seacliff district, called the *Humanist House*. The lively young group of humanists living in the mansion were glad to babysit the rock. The tall and stately house, complete with an iron gate and a long sweeping driveway, had a garage with two large swinging doors that the *Neprhipod* could just barely fit in.

The *Humanist House* people were excited about the jade. One visitor went down alone to look at it and when he had not returned in over two hours his friends went to see what had happened and found him sound asleep, sprawled out on top of the jade, succumbed to the calming powers of the massive stone. Then there was a message we found taped to a fender when we opened the doors to put some last minute paint touches on the jade trailer. Louise Colburn, a guitar player and singer, had seen the jade, made up a song about it, and left her name in case we were interested. I called her, and in exchange for a ride to Berkeley, where she had a singing engagement, she said she would sit on the rock and sing her jade song in Chinatown. Since she was good looking, Gary offered to give her a ride to Berkeley. It didn't work out, however, since she got laryngitis and Gary got two flat tires, and neither one of them showed up. The last we heard of her she was singing her jade song in a New York nightclub.

There was also a visiting topless waitress who scrutinized the rock carefully and then said, "Oh, what I wouldn't give to be balled on that rock!"

Gary began to fade into the background. He had met a ballet dancer and was working hard to save enough money to accompany her to Europe. "Besides," he said, "the people thing is for you and Jim."

We prepared the *Nephripod* for its debut. We removed all its chains, and Jim welded five 2½ inch pipes on the sled, angled up from the corners to the rock. The pipes were painted gold, and we lined the bed

DON WOBBER AND JIM NORTON
They polished their $180,000 stone

A Find Off Monterey

The Giant Gem From Jade Cove

By Peter Stack

Getting the rock — wresting it from the churning cold sea where it had loomed in a secret cave for centuries was the singular obsession of four strangely dedicated men.

The rock is jade, an enthralling hunk of gem weighing almost five tons. Its owners claim it is the largest piece of jade on the continent. Its value: $180,000.

From the sheer cliffs along the coast of Monterey county, the four men fastened their gazes on the waters below. They knew the rock was there. That was in November, when preliminary exploration began.

raised with floats and, towed behind an outboard-powered raft, it was prodded onto a rocky beach near Gorda.

During the underwater operation, Wobber said, his colleagues learned of a plot to pirate the boulder.

"We did some checking, a lot of checking." Wobber said. They rolled into Monterey, searching for the pirates. They examined and re-examined boats all along the coast any vessel with a salvage boom capable of lifting the rock from the brine.

"There weren't any boats that could handle it." Wobber said. "We were satisfied the pirates would never be able to pull it off without meeting us on the scene."

of the sled and the wooden fenders of the trailer with bright red carpet. We then painted the jade trailer blue. When it was towed by the red and white Bronco, the *Nephripod* in its red, gold, and blue setting couldn't help but attract attention.

Now we were ready for the press. I called the *San Francisco Chronicle*, told them the story of how we got the *Nephripod* from the ocean, and said that we were taking the rock to Chinatown to check out the reaction. The *Chronicle* not only sent a photographer, they did a feature story on the *Nephripod*.

Our story was on the wire! Reported not only nationwide but all over the world! We were famous! The Philippine papers said we had discovered the jade off the west coast of Africa. Newspapers in Mexico City said the stone was worth over a million dollars.

People liked the story. Sandwiched in among the gloomy newspaper reports of rape, murder, wars, and rising prices, our story was refreshing, like a fresh sea breeze blowing across their morning coffee. They liked it because it meant that people were still out there dealing directly with nature. It was a story of rugged individualism, a story that smacked of hope and inspiration and idealism.

In Chinatown people crowded around the rock, touching and rubbing it, asking questions. There were interviews, TV cameras, and a camera crew I had lined up. There was a feeling of excitement in the air, almost a certain madness. People who had read the story in the newspaper came to talk to us and to see and touch the great stone.

Everyone was curious. What was it worth? Where did we get it? How did we get it out of the ocean? What would we do with it? Old people, young people, all nationalities and colors came to rub and touch the jade.

Kem Lee, a Chinese-American photographer, arranged for several pretty Chinese girls to pose on top of the *Nephripod*. To get a low camera angle he lay in the middle of Grant Avenue on his back instructing the girls to "rub the rock, rub the rock!" while he took pictures. Cars piled up, traffic snarled, horns sounded. But Kem was oblivious to all distractions until he was through shooting.

Later Kem Lee opened his shirt, reached beneath his undershirt, and pulled out an ancient piece of jade that he wore around his neck. It was smooth and flat, shaped like a hatchet blade. It had been used for digging roots 3000 years ago by a Chinese herb doctor. Kem Lee said he would never take it off and wouldn't trade it even for our rock!

To get movie footage we drove down to the financial district, where I had worked what seemed a long, long time ago. How different it all looked now from the front seat of Jim's Bronco, towing our jade canoe!

At one point a group of five Chinese businessmen from Taiwan, dressed in immaculate black suits, stopped us in the middle of the street, holding up traffic while they inspected the rock. Amid angry shouts from truck drivers and other motorists one of the businessmen came up to me and said in perfect English, "I have never seen anything like your jade in my life. It is a most beautiful stone. You should be proud of it."

I later asked Jim, "Well, now do you believe that the Chinese are emotional?"

"It's hard to believe," he said, "But I guess they can be."

Back in Chinatown we overheard some teenagers say, "That can't be jade. It's too big."

Near the end of the day a huge truck pulled alongside us. The driver leaned out of the cab, looked down at the jade and the crowd around it, and yelled to us, "Hey, remember me?"

I looked up at him, "Sure I do."

He shouted to the crowd, "I'm the first guy that rubbed the rock when it came to Chinatown this morning!" Then he waved to the crowd, put his truck in gear and left.

I gave a piece of jade from the Cove to a Chinese friend, Nanying Stella Wong. She wrote a poem about it:

> You brought me
> jade
> Han-smooth,
> Sung-bold,
> tore it
> with your own
> hands from cave
> under turning sea
> placed it deep in
> churning green of me.
> Not rock, with carved
> peach of longevity,
> nor etched stone of
> pomegranate continuity
> —you gave me jade glow!
> Born of ocean,
> variegated veins
> my veins,
> translucence,
> my view.
> I shall return it polished
> between voyages.

On our way home cars pulled up alongside the Bronco, windows rolled down and occupants shouted the now familiar, "Is that the rock?" A girl in a sports car, pulling out of a side street, spotted us passing and roared up on the driver's side a few minutes later. She asked, "What is that beautiful rock?" When Jim told her it was jade, she said, "Out of sight! Out of sight!" and sped off. A bearded man on a motorcycle came alongside. He had a tinted glass shield attached to his helmet, so his face was not visible. From out of this armor came a deep voice, "Is that the rock?"

A man in a red VW camper pulled up, asked Jim some questions and finally followed us all the way to Seacliff. We thought he was either a nut or a reporter—or a rockhound. When we finally got to *Humanist House* he told us he was an archeologist. He talked about how he had located the lost city of Atlantis and said he would like us to go with him to collect artifacts. It was in the Bahamas, he said. There were some ruins underwater close to shore, and many divers were getting gold artifacts from the site, but the papers were suppressing the news. He didn't offer to bankroll the trip, however.

There was a small group of people who did not react so favorably to the newspaper story; they were members of the State Lands Commission, called back from vacation for a special meeting.

On August 5, a Mr. Smith from the Lands Commission telephoned Jim. He asked if we had a permit to take jade out of the ocean. Jim told him we didn't. Jim explained that ours wasn't the first boulder to come out of the area. Thousands of rockhounds had been collecting rocks along the beaches for years, and no one was aware that permits were required.

Mr. Smith said that if we had no permit the rock belonged to the State. We would be hearing from them again directly.

In spite of the State of California we needed one more day in Chinatown to complete our film. While I was upset about the State's claim, I tried to remain optimistic. I rationalized that Mr. Smith was probably a little man in a minor position who had just been jumped on by his boss and obviously didn't know the facts about traditional rock collecting at Jade Cove. I hoped that nothing would come of it.

As soon as we drove the rock into the street the celebration started all over again, and we forgot about the State. We had been on all the local television channels the night before and now everyone seemed to know us. We drove along Lombard Street among cheers and greetings from everyone we passed. It was like being in a movie!

We went to Chinatown again, and just as on the previous day, people who had seen the rock before wanted their friends, lovers, wives, relatives to see it. On Montgomery Street in the Financial District we shot some footage of three small Chinese boys who ran alongside the trailer for six blocks. Then Larry Booth, our film-maker, sat on the back of the jade trailer and shot forward across the jade, using a fisheye lens. (In the finished film the rock bouncing along beneath the tall buildings almost seems to be alive.)

Larry was inspired and wanted to get the rock to a place where he could shoot it in the late afternoon sunlight, unobstructed by shadows, a place where we could turn it around and pick up some of its more interesting lines. We decided to go to the parking lot of the Yacht Harbor in the Marina District.

When we had parked, a yachtsman came up and scrutinized the rock carefully. He said that to him the *Nephripod* represented every wave he had ever seen at sea. He showed me how if you looked across the rock when the sun hit it at a certain angle it gave the appearance of ripples on the surface of the sea. Another area looked like a huge breaker folding over, poised, about to break, as though frozen in action. In some places the jade depicted a profile of swells on a stormy sea, and from a certain angle, when the sun hit them obliquely, the crests of these "waves" glowed transparent green like real waves when the sun lights them from behind.

Our cameraman's wife, Sheila, put her feelings this way: "You know, it's funny, but I've had a feeling all day that this rock is alive. It's as if it knows about us, like it's aware that we're little transient conscious-nesses running around it and picking it up and carrying it around and rubbing it and feeling it. Things like that are just a wink in the eye of time, and this rock goes on and on. Long after the United States falls down the rock will be there, maybe in the Smithsonian, or what once was the Smithsonian, just sitting there, being eternal."

The next day Jim got an official letter from the Bureau of Lands, claiming that the jade belonged to the State.

We went to the State Division of Mines in the Ferry Building. The officials said they knew of no rules about taking jade, but they suggested we get an attorney.

We chose Cliff Kruger, who was head of the committee putting on the San Francisco Gem and Mineral Show. Kruger suggested that we lay low for a while; the less publicity we got the better. He said that the State would not take the rock from us physically. "People would rise up in arms against that sort of thing."

Later, I phoned my wife, who was out of town, and told her about the day's activities. I mentioned that I had got a call from Buck, an old friend, who had been in touch with Robert McCloskey, Public Relations Director of the U.S. Department of State. He had suggested to McCloskey that President Nixon might buy the *Nephripod* from us and give it to Chairman Mao in China. He said that McCloskey seemed en-thusiastic about the idea and was going to call back. "Buck just called

McCloskey up," I told my wife. "He was in public relations in the army, so he knows the ins and outs of it. Can you imagine the government giving the jade to China? They'd love it! And the U.S. Government would just tell the State to go screw themselves. They'd be fighting over our rock!

"I called Larry Booth and told him about the call to the State Department. He nearly had a fit laughing.

"We could sell the film for a fortune! My God, we'd have international publicity. You know, it's like a grade B movie. It's too much. But it's just crazy enough to happen. Who knows?

"Send me a file in a cake," I said as I hung up.

31. ROCK SHOW

$180,000 JADE FIND STATE PROPERTY?
—Bakersfield Californian

STATE MAY CLAIM $180,000 IN JADE PULLED FROM OCEAN
—Los Angeles Times

4½ TON DISPUTE—STATE GREEN WITH ENVY
—San Francisco Examiner

STATE AFTER 4 DIVERS WHO FOUND JADE ROCK
—San Francisco Chronicle

On August 11, newspapers all over the world carried the story of our dispute with the State of California over the *Nephripod*. We were trespassers, criminals! It was a trial without jury by the news media. No paper bothered to tell our side of the story.

At a meeting in Sacramento the State Lands Commission decided that we were guilty. The *San Francisco Examiner* quoted Mr. Everitts, Assistant Executive of the Lands Commission, as saying: "... if the huge rock came from State waters it belongs to the State."

Thus began fourteen months of agony, fourteen months during which we were harassed and even lied to by the State of California.

Sonny was not involved because he had already sold his 10% share to us for $2,500. Gary was curious about the proceedings, but he did not want to get involved. Jim and I, however, decided to fight it out. Jim was seriously worried and I was too. My optimistic nature would allow me to forget our problems on the surface, but my smoldering temper erupted Vesuvius-like from time to time. We were not always morose, of course; we laughed, worked, and even partied occasionally.

I went on with my studies and often lost myself in my animals by slipping beneath the cold, forgiving waters of Monterey Bay. Life went on, but the dark, ominous cloud hung over us, and it was not good.

In preparation for the Gem and Mineral Show we kept the rock under guard at the Hall of Flowers in Golden Gate Park, where the Show was to be held. I got some free passes to the Show for the people at *Humanist House,* so I dropped by and gave them to one of the residents to distribute. I told him we hadn't located a permanent place for the rock and asked if he thought the *Humanists* would mind, after all the bad publicity, if we returned the rock to their garage after the Show. He assured me they would like to have it back, adding: "I notice it's been foggy out here ever since you took the rock away from us."

The morning before the Show was to open a man knocked on the door of the Hall of Flowers. He asked for Jim, who was helping some of his old cronies set up booths. He identified himself as an employee of the Federal Government (probably of the Bureau of Internal Revenue). He wanted to know about the other rocks we had taken, what had happened to them, had we reported their disposition and the income we had received from them? Jim told him we had donated two to museums and had not sold any of them.

It looked as though from then on the State and Federal Governments would follow every move we made.

Our attorney set a meeting with the State for after the Gem and Mineral Show. He advised us not to tell anyone where we had found the rock.

Jim asked, "What does it matter? We have nothing to hide!"

I told him we had better follow our attorney's advice, but then I wavered, as Jim, his mind set like a compass, convinced me: after all, we had nothing to hide. Whatever happened to truth and integrity, to people who follow their dreams? Not wanting to face the legal cobwebs that were beginning to entangle us, I longed to jump in the VW and head down the coast, to breathe free air again. But this was just the beginning of our new problems.

Soon we were overwhelmed by people again. They understood, the people understood! At the Gem Show Jim and I stood by the *Nephripod,* telling about our adventure and encouraging people to feel and admire the rock. Almost everyone we met was upset about the State's claim. Thousands of them had been to Jade Cove and collected there themselves. There were many voices:

An old lady with a cane came up to me, "Darn it, I get so mad! Fight for it, fight for it! All right boys, you just fight for it!"

Another lady chimed in, "I just hope the government doesn't take any of this away from you. That would be one of the rottenest tricks I can imagine."

A six-foot-three man looked at the 9,000 pound rock, then down at us and mumbled, "I thought you guys would be much bigger than you are."

Jim and I lapped it up. There was great joy, and there was great concern. The people were on our side. Most of the people we talked to thought that the State was in the wrong and that we should circulate a petition. The rockhounds would back us, and skin divers and other people too.

Later Jim said he had been told that the Gem Show would probably break all attendance records because of the *Nephripod*. (It did.) One man had read about our "million dollar jade find" in a Mexican newspaper and had made a special trip from Mexico City just to see it.

In the center of all this talk and concern sat the *Nephripod*. Thousands of people came to rub and touch it. Things happened around it.

During his break the ticket-taker came up to me. "I can't believe what I just saw," he said. "There was a woman standing here a few minutes ago. She was just standing here with her hands on the rock. And she had a funny look in her eyes. Glazed. She turned to her husband and she said, 'Honey, I ain't never going to forget this rock.' And she kept saying it; she said it about four times, 'I ain't never going to forget this rock, never going to forget this rock.' She had her hands on it, like she was welded to it, see." He put his hands on the *Nephripod* to demonstrate.

I'll never forget one woman, who saw the rock as she entered the gate. Her eyes lit up, and with a strange smile on her face she put her hands out in front of her like a sleepwalker and floated over to the rock, as though she was in a trance. When her hands touched the rock she stood there and caressed it, with her eyes closed and the ecstatic smile still on her face.

The rock show, like our adventure in Chinatown, had become a special celebration. Perhaps many people who touched the *Nephripod* had in some way rediscovered a sense of their own beginnings, and had made contact with that lost and primitive part of the self that resides within each of us as a sort of universal subconscious. The jade seemed to have a special meaning that couldn't be vocalized—and didn't have to be.

I recalled the long, sensitive fingers of Tarkin as his hands explored the smooth surfaces of this huge piece of jade for the first time. As I looked at the rock in the Hall of Flowers, sunlight slanting across it in the fading afternoon, and at the people caressing it the murmur of their voices seemed strangely like the murmur of a distant and ancient sea....

At that moment it all seemed truly magic!

32. PIRATES BY LAND

A LETTER TO the *Los Angeles Times* published on August 23, 1971, said: "I hope that I am not the only reader indignant at and disgusted with the reported actions of a 2-by-4 state bureaucrat, supposedly a public servant, in trying to get the five-ton block of jade away from the four divers who found it in the ocean. These men showed a great deal of ingenuity and worked hard to get the result they did. There was a time when these qualities were admired, instead of being sniped at by the small fry."

*   *   *

We were in our attorney's office with a mineral engineer, a state geologist, and Virgil Butler, Associate Counsel for the State Lands Commission.

Jim was saying, "All right then, we'll put the rock back in the ocean where we got it." He meant it, and he was speaking for both of us.

Virgil Butler tilted forward. His face was red, his neck bulging inside his starched white collar. "If you do, I'll have you up on criminal charges. It would be the same as destroying State property!"

In answer to our attorney's statement that traditionally Jade Cove had been open to thousands of rock collectors, Butler proclaimed: "Then there have been 10,000 trespassers, but that doesn't make them innocent. The State has criminal statutes and can use them."

Butler wanted us to agree to certain things or face the State in court: 1) We would have to apply to the Corps of Engineers immediately for "permission to take the rock;" 2) We would have to apply for a prospector's permit; 3) We could not physically change the rock or we would be convicted of altering State property; 4) We would have to comply with the State's demand to let them look at the rock (no one from the State had yet seen it). Also, they would have to evaluate *it* before making a decision as to what to do with *us*.

After the meeting, the state geologist and the mineral engineer followed us to *Humanist House,* where we swung open the garage doors to let them inspect the rock. The geologist, Charles Chesterman, a very knowledgeable and likable man, explained the problem of establishing value: even jade experts in the Orient estimating uncut Burmese jade can make or lose fortunes, because it is impossible to tell what a stone is like inside. Practically speaking, he said, there was no way to determine the value of the *Nephripod* without the State slicing it or running a core into it.

The state engineer looked like a skinny Red Skelton. He wore a tight-fitting suit, a matching green tie, and pointed high-topped shoes. He snapped Polaroid pictures of the rock, all of which came out bad. After each picture he tossed wastepapers dripping with chemicals on the driveway. Jim and I picked up the papers and put them in the Bronco, and I chided him about being an ecological disaster.

From *Humanist House* he was going to Jade Cove to photograph the site. I could picture him tippy-toeing so that he wouldn't get mud on his fancy shoes, peering down at the ocean, trying desperately to imagine our rock through the water, and then strewing paper all over the cliffs. His presence at the Cove would clearly profane that beautiful landscape, just as the State was now profaning our adventure with their accusations.

That night Jim telephoned me to tell me how complicated the prospector's permit requirements were. They wanted a survey map of the area we had found the rock in, copies of our birth certificates, environmental impact reports, and more. He also said that during the prospecting phase the State gets 20% of everything recovered, whether the minerals are kept, sold, or donated. If we followed these procedures we would be operating as if we were commercial miners or oil companies.

By August 30 our attorney had the prospector's permit papers ready. Jim and I now agreed, however, that if we got a permit we would establish a precedent that would be unfair to other rockhounds, since we would then be the only ones in the Big Sur who could collect legally. We decided not to sign.

Gary suggested that we switch to his lawyer, Terry Androlini. Since both lawyers were donating their time for The Cause, we made the switch.

On September 2 the Assistant Attorney General, J. Shavelson, telephoned Terry that he had to appear before a Legislative Committee and said that the State wanted an interim agreement that would prevent both parties from taking legal action, revokable with 15 days written notice. Also, he said that the State wanted us to: (1) Promise not to take the rock out of the State. (2) Suspend the statute of limitations while negotiating. (3) Post a $15,000 bond.

We agreed only to item (1).

The State, afraid that we would disappear with our rock or otherwise embarrass them, wanted to know how reputable we were. I told Terry Androlini that I was only a student and, as such, had no visible means of support. Having nothing more substantial to say I added that my grandfather had been Police Commissioner of San Francisco. I felt like the proverbial minister's daughter with a bad reputation around town. Jim, having quit his job and not even being eligible for unemployment insurance, was currently looking for work, with two strikes against him—his age and his eyesight. We described him as being retired. It was a surprise to all of us when Gary turned out to be the most reputable; he was the only one who was employed!

On September 3 we drafted a *Petition to Protect Freelance Rock Collecting.* Over 3,000 people signed it.

Our next meeting with Virgil Butler, J. Shavelson, and another Assistant Attorney General began placidly enough; we all shook hands as though we were taking part in an international peace conference. Butler opened by saying that he had not yet received our request for a prospector's permit. Very calmly, I told him we were not going to file because of the moral implications.

"What?" His face reddened and he began to quiver all over as he sprang to the edge of his chair. "If we had known that we would have taken a different line of action! We would have seized the rock on the basis that you were running an illegal commercial operation!"

"We were not running a commercial operation!" I shot back.

"No one who was not operating commercially would spend so much money getting a rock!" he retorted.

"That's not so. If a rockhound finds a rock a hundred miles back in the boondocks, once he's committed to getting that rock he gets it out some way. We started out with surplus lifting bags and inexpensive gear. We couldn't help the difficulties we had. We lost a lot of equipment when the sea got rough. We didn't say, 'We're going to invest X-number of dollars.' But the more trouble we had the more equipment, money, and time we had to pour in."

Terry Androlini added, "If they had done it commercially, they would have brought in a boat and pulled it out in three days, but they wanted to comply with the rules down there as they understood them."

The charge that bringing out the *Nephripod* was a commercial operation was a recurring theme we were to hear often. It fit some image of us Butler was trying to form.

One Assistant Attorney General asked the other Assistant Attorney General, "If this was such a big operation, how is it the State was unaware of what was going on? Why didn't our men see these guys before this?"

"It was not a big operation," I explained. "We looked like everyone else down there. We used garden hoes to dig with. We carried all the gear down on our backs."

They had a hard time grasping this concept. When I mentioned other rocks we had taken, Terry brought out a collection of articles in books, magazines, and journals about these and other jade finds and asked, "Why wasn't there any State action on what has evidently been a customary and well-publicized practice for thousands of Californians before your action on our rock?"

The reply was that action was instigated because our find had achieved wide publicity. Therefore, it sounded as if getting publicity was our crime.

Terry told them that we wanted to tie the settlement on our rock to future legislation in order to protect all rockhounds—so that the State couldn't put others through the same kind of run-around we were getting.

Shavelson demanded that we reinstate our interim agreement by agreeing that the statute of limitations would be suspended while the case was being argued. Terry was adamant. "No way! As far as we're concerned, since my clients' equipment was on the rock over a year ago, the statute of limitations has already run out. Theoretically, the rock has been in their possession for a year."

This visibly shook them up. The meeting ended with us promising that we would look over some additional items the State wanted us to agree to and would let them know our reaction.

Two weeks later Jim and I walked down the halls of the State Capital building in Sacramento, our shoes echoing on the smooth marble floors. We entered a large, overheated meeting room where 30 to 40 people, most of them in suits, sat in theaterlike rows. Up front was a stage with a podium, table and chairs, microphones, and recording equipment.

The meeting began with K. Cory, Chairman of the Joint Committee on Public Domain, asking Mr. Hortig, Executive Officer of the State Lands Commission, to speak.

Hortig's eloquent voice rang out. "As your committee is aware, pursuant to the request at the last hearing that you made reference to, a summary report was transmitted for the information of the committee as to the status of the followup in connection with the jade find, which in brief form resulted in a complete understanding on the part of the finders of the jade that it is the property of the State of California, and the execution of an interim..."

The Chairman interrupted. "Pardon me..."

"Yes?"

"In reference to Exhibit Two, the document they signed, or that their attorney signed, determined that the interim agreement shall not be interpreted as an admission that the State has any legal interest in this discovery..."

"This has now been..."

"Has it gone beyond that point?"

"Well, partially, Chairman Cory, in this sense. On September 15, last week, a supplement to this agreement was signed. Also in signing the supplement a new attorney has entered on behalf of Wobber and Norton, who removed the jade from Monterey Bay, and it was agreed, and the language is being worked on today, that first there will be added to the existing agreement an agreement that the statute of limitations, and similar defenses will not apply for the period from the signing of the interim agreement to any time that has terminated as a result of other agreements, prospecting permits, or whatever, being entered into by these people, and additionally..."

Of course, the statements Hortig made were simply not true. Either he deliberately lied or this $28,000-per-year employee was misinformed.

The rest of the meeting was taken up with the history of Jade Cove "according to Hortig."

I followed the plight of a fly which, trapped in the meeting hall, had found its own small world on the head of a bald man dozing a few seats in front of me. The man was making a feeble effort to keep the fly away with his right hand, although the fly's pattern centered around the left side of his cranium. I thought of how the seaweed piled up on the shore of the Cove covered the bald rocks, and of the kelp flies buzzing over it, and of the incessant lapping of the waves on the shore... It was all I could do to keep awake.

Before the meeting closed Chairman Cory called for comments from the floor. I got up and stated that I did not agree in general with Mr. Hortig in regard to our find at Jade Cove.

Cory replied, "Mr. Wobber, I'm not sure what the public policy is in regard to rock collecting but what disturbs me is that we don't seem to *have* a public policy."

He continued. "This is our basic course: we are picking on your jade find to highlight the fact that we don't have a policy, and I think it's high time we got one."

Cory insisted that the State Lands Division come up with recommendations for future legislation by the time of their next meeting, January 1st, but his words and the tone of his voice indicated that he had little faith that any solutions would be presented.

After the meeting, Don Everitts of the State Lands Division, a rock collector himself, told us that they were having a hard time coming up with ideas to control future rock collecting and would welcome suggestions.

Subsequently, we talked to several gem and mineral clubs, but we found that many members were reluctant to get involved with issues that might be political, because the clubs might lose their non-profit tax advantage. This viewpoint seemed ridiculous: if collecting was banned on state land there would be so little land left to collect on that the clubs would have to be abandoned anyway.

Although we had passed one barrier—the State no longer insisted on a prospecting permit—the State, like a huge, impersonal octopus, was slowly drawing us into its "Great Machinery of Legal Fabrication and Justification for Past Action," without regard for the very real circumstances of the present situation. Although we had tried, we evidently lost the ability to communicate with them—as if they were organisms from another planet. I kept mulling over Cory's words: the idea that the State needed to "pick on our rock" to instigate legislation really stuck in my craw.

The Attorney General's office (Virgil Butler and company) had one purpose: to protect the State from abuses, real or imagined. The fact that our case did not fit existing law was not the point. They were not interested in individual rights, morality, justice, innocence, or guilt.

They had plenty of money to throw around, and they were not afraid to use it. They spent at least $80,000 on our case.

Time and time again they threatened court action, knowing we would lose more money than we could afford—even if we won. Along with Chairman Cory, we felt that there "was no public policy in this area." But if that was the case, how could we, the public, have violated policy? There was something illogical, grotesquely inane, about the whole process. We felt they should drop charges. However, we were willing to negotiate a reasonable settlement, not because we were guilty but in order to get out of the steel trap from which we could see no escape.

There were further meetings, and it looked as if the case might drag on forever. Assuming that we might be able to settle our differences by talking to the State on a person-to-person basis, we let Terry Androlini go—keeping him in the background, however, to help us if we got into trouble.

I began to feel that going to court might be more honorable than the kind of phony sparring around we had been doing. If we did go to court Jim and I would fight the State alone and without counsel. This vision of the two of us battling the Great Machinery of the State of California was appealing.

A few days after notiying the State that we were without counsel I received a letter from my newly acquired enemy, Virgil Butler, in which he implied that our exhibiting the rock in a recent antique show and in a public park in Oakland was an effort "to gain greater publicity so that income may be received in the future." We must have disappointed Butler when we reported that we hadn't made one dime.

After seven days of filling my wastebasket with lengthy and vindictive replies to Butler I decided to telephone Shavelson. I told him that Butler's actions were creating a greater rift, not helping to solve mutual problems. Shavelson expressed a desire to settle on a friendly basis. He said he felt we should let each other know where we stood on things, that we should, "let our hair down." I told him that as a taxpayer I would rely on him to protect my interests. In reply he said that he would keep me aware of the legality of both sides, but he added that because it was his job, his interest had to lie with the State.

Soon, in the spirit of our new relationship, he insisted that we sign another agreement—an agreement which carried the same old statute of limitations waiver, the signing of which would mean that the State could shelve our case forever. We refused to sign.

On November 1, 1971 an informal meeting was called in San Francisco to work out plans for a peaceful out-of-court settlement. Shavelson, Butler, Everitts, and Al Willard, another Assistant Attorney General, were there.

The State proposed the following settlement possibilities—without offering to put them in writing, however: (1) Go to court. (2) Pay the State $2,000 (based on assumed extraction costs). (3) Give the rock outright to a State institution. (4) Pay the State 20 percent of the rock's value. (5) Put the rock in a State building on public display for a year and give four lectures with movies, free to the public, during that period of time.

We told them that only Plan Five was acceptable. I said I would check on the Moss Landing Marine Laboratory and San Francisco State University as possible display-lecture sites.

They had found out the amount we had paid Sonny for his share of the *Nephripod,* a figure they subsequently used in evaluating the rock, but fortunately they didn't ask what percent he had owned, nor did we volunteer the information. They also learned I had a temper.

Butler tried to establish the *Nephripod's* value by how much it had cost to extract it. With rising anger, I went through my "rockhound commitment" song and dance routine again, concluding with, "Jim lost an eye on our expedition. What's that worth to you bastards?"

To their old "court threat" tactics I replied that we would fight them in court alone, without counsel, just as we had fought to get our rock out of the ocean. And we would win!

Butler, cocksure and smug, said "You won't win. You trespassed on State Land!"

A week later, by telephone, Shavelson said that Plan Two would cost us $2,500 and that if we decided on Plan Five we would have to pay the State money in addition to giving free lectures. He wouldn't tell me how much, however. So he had changed all terms of settlement agreed to in the San Francisco meeting.

I had already talked to the head librarian at San Francisco State University about exhibiting the rock there. Now I would have to go back and tell him that the State had changed its mind.

The State seemed to have proved beyond any doubt that it did not want to negotiate.

I polished the *Nephripod* for about two hours to calm myself, then banged out a short letter to Shavelson:

"Before we can talk any further to State institutions about your proposal of displaying the rock and giving public lectures on their premises, we need something in writing indicating that the State's obligations in this matter are sincere, and that this is a serious proposal."

33. REVERBERATIONS

I CALLED JIM and suggested that we take a trip, to get away from our troubles for a while. We decided to combine our retreat with a trip to the U. S. Forestry Regional Headquarters in King City, so that we could get the Federal Government's viewpoint on the State's rights at the Cove.

The head ranger, who had served at the same post since 1942, told us that the Forestry Service had built and improved the paths down to Jade Cove beach so that people could collect. He added that just the other day he had received a phone call from the State Lands Commission asking if his rangers would reinforce State collecting laws—a call that had, no doubt, been instigated by our rock. He told them that he had no intention of doing so.

The caller also said that the State owned all lands from "average *low* tide out to three miles." We questioned this, because the State had told us that they controlled from mean *high* tide out to three miles. But the ranger said he had had the State man repeat the information, and was told a second time that the land boundry was figured from average low tide. (The State was obviously confused as to what the boundaries were, because we later confirmed that "mean high tide" was correct. Mean high tide is a rather nebulous border at any rate and not one that the average rockhound, miner, or anyone else can define with any certainty, because when the contour of a beach shifts, the mean high tide line shifts also. Because the State is continually gaining and losing land in this manner, the shifting borderlines would lead to disputes if there should be a question of the exact location of a given rock).

We then went to see Ralph Gould, who had been a ranger at Jade Cove for years but had since retired. He was mad as hell at the State for their action against us. He said he used to give campfire lectures telling tourists how and where to collect jade from California beaches and said that the Plaskett camping grounds had quadrupled in size in the last eight years in order to accommodate the increasing number of rockhounds.

Ralph also told us a story about Jade Cove during the Second World War, when much of the Big Sur coast was controlled by the army. The major who was in command had a helicopter at his disposal and was not adverse to using it for his personal needs. For example, he wanted a lemon tree in front of his house, so he had his men fly to an abandoned ranch in the back country, ball up the roots of an old lemon tree and lift it out by helicopter.

The major was also interested in jade. He used to have his men gather jade on the beach for their recreation, then he would have them lift it off the shore by helicopter. He began to get greedy and even had them dynamiting the cliffs for jade too.

One day he caught a fisherman picking up jade on the beach and had him arrested for trespassing. He said that the reason he didn't want any civilians at Jade Cove was because the Army was shooting over the road. It is strictly illegal to shoot over a public road, so the fisherman took his case higher up, and in the shuffle of the cards it came out that the major had not only been shooting over the Coast Highway, but had also used an Army helicopter to fly out the lemon tree and to take jade off the beach. The major was shipped out in a hurry, and shortly thereafter the Army moved up in the mountains where they could have a safe target range, and the Forestry Service took over on the coast.

Finally, we drove over to the coast at Cambria and visited several local rock shop owners on the homeward leg of the trip. They said that people in that economically depressed area were concerned about the State's action since much of their livelihood depended upon the summer rockhound and tourist trade. We dropped by Sonny's house to tell him not to talk to anyone from the State—except to refer them to us. Sonny wasn't there, so we talked to his sister. We told her that the State now wanted 20 percent of the airplane Sonny had bought with the money we had paid him for his share of the *Nephripod*. She said with a touch of alarm, "Don't tell Sonny or he'll head for the bush country and never come out again."

34. PIRATES REDUX

THE STATE, not satisfied with their geologist's first report, was sending him back.

I flipped the garage lights on. There it lay, gleaming and bright. "I'm sorry, old *Nephripod*," I said as I slipped the carpeting out from around it, tucked the bright red material in a cardboard box, and hid it back in a corner. I mixed a bucket of hot water and detergent and washed the rock down. While the rock was still wet, I shook dusty carpets over it. By the time Chesterman arrived the *Nephripod* was dry, dull, and disreputable.

Chesterman again explained the problem of evaluating the jade without taking a core sample. Another fruitless visit.

A week later, Everitts dropped by with a request that we submit "extraction expenses"—the amount of money it had cost us to take the *Nephripod* out of the ocean. The figures we finally submitted, however, were evidently too low to contribute to whatever predetermined settlement scheme was in the State's mind.*

By December, four months after our first contact with the State, no substantial progress was evident. I now sent off a seven-page, single-spaced typewritten letter to Everitts, outlining our frustrations. After receiving my letter the State maintained an ominous 2½ month silence. The public meeting Cory had set for January was cancelled. In February I sent a follow-up letter, pointing out that since I had received no reply to my two previous letters I assumed that the State was letting our case "die a natural death." I mentioned that the rock had been on display several times in conjunction with free lectures to the public, and thus, in essence, we had complied with one of the settlement proposals suggested at the San Francisco meeting.

A month later Virgil Butler replied in his usual style suggesting we get together to discuss the rock's "final disposition." He suggested that I should come to see him "if you should happen to be in the Los Angeles area," or, he continued, "I will give you a call the first time I am able to be in the San Francisco Bay area." It all sounded so damned casual. He had blithely brushed away all my letter writing and the frustrations stated in my December letter with a statement that "many letters have been written."

---

*Failing other methods of establishing a value for the *Nephripod,* the State finally decided to base it on the $2,500 we had paid Sonny for his 10 percent—which they thought was actually 25 percent. This method of evaluation made as much sense as anything else they did. The State's description of this is interesting: "Several authorities have examined it and appraisals range from its being valueless as gem material up to a maximum of $10,000. Most agree its chief value lies in being kept intact and used as a museum attraction."

We were not certain just who the several authorities who examined the rock were; we knew of only one: Chesterman.

On July 11, 1974, I received a professional independent estimate from Paul F. Patchick, AIPG, a geologist and mineralogist of high reputation. Describing the *Nephripod* as an extraordinary specimen, he placed a conservative evaluation on it of $500 per pound, or $4,500,000.

I decided to hell with it. We were not about to go through any more shenanigans with Butler and tribe. We would not get together again. My mounting anger led me to contact Karrol Maughmer in Southern California, a woman who had been upset about our case and who had indicated that she "would alert some elected legislators to the facts in this case." It was a last-ditch effort.

Somehow the pressure Karrol exerted instigated an immediate appointment with Butler, who came to my house. He seemed miraculously transformed when he entered: somewhat wilted, and much smaller of stature than I remembered. Jim, Butler, my wife, and I sat around a kitchen table; the adversary was now sipping coffee with us.

Butler gathered himself together to present a lengthy diatribe on the State Lands Commission's structure, position, and responsibility. Among other things, he confirmed that the State's evaluation was based on the payment to Sonny. After this 25-minute monologue, he launched into an elaborate outline of settlement possibilities.

I had noticed the tip of an envelope sticking out of his inside coat pocket. Bored with being lectured at, I jumped gleefully from my chair and pointed to the envelope. "Does your visit have something to do with what's in your pocket? Is that something we should read?"

At last I knew we had a victory!

Was this diminished bureaucrat, the adversary, the man I had feared? I felt almost sorry for him. The transparent veneer of pomp no longer hid the man I thought I knew.

"Well, uh, yes it is," he said, recovering. "You see, I'm a practical attorney, and I'm always prepared."

Yes, I felt sorry for him. Yet I couldn't forget our previous dealings when the shoe had been on the other foot.

He took the envelope out of his pocket, slowly, reluctantly. It contained the rough draft of a letter the State wanted us to send to them. The State recommended that we pay $500 cash and list as expenses the approximately $2,000 it had cost us to extract, exhibit, and store the *Nephripod*.

Before Butler left we gave him our written suggestion that a three-member board be established, with one representative from the State Lands Commission, one from rockhound clubs, and one from environmental groups. This board would act to prevent or regulate collecting in areas that became a problem because of the removal of too many rocks. Such areas would be posted and specific regulations about them would be announced through clubs and the media. All areas would be "free" unless they became problem areas.

When Butler had gone we called Terry for his advice. Then we made revisions, signed the letter and sent it off. Settlement now seemed imminent, so I thanked our "concerned party," Karrol Maughmer, reporting that, since it looked as if settlement were just around the corner, no further action would be necessary.

To my surprise, a few days later I received a copy of an official memo Butler had sent to the State Lands Commission which contained our recommendation for the control of rockhounding. At last we were the good guys.

A month later, J. Smith, called back into the case to "clean it up," asked us to modify the settlement proposal by submitting a list of only those expenses we had incurred in exhibiting the rock for *public benefit*. Such expenses would be deducted from the $2,000 settlement figure the State had decided on, $2,000 being 20 percent of the $10,000 value they had set on the *Nephripod*. So we drummed up $1,500 worth of "expenses," including our labor at $3.50 an hour—an arbitrary wage we arrived at to make the figures come our right for the State.

The next meeting was to be on the August calendar. The August meeting didn't take place, so in September I phoned Smith to find out when we would be on the agenda. Since I thought time had run out (it had been over a year since the State had first claimed the *Nephripod*), I also asked him to let me know the wording of the statute of limitations clause on minerals. He said it might be weeks before he could answer the agenda question, but he would call right back on the statute of limitations.

Smith didn't call back on either count. Since over five months had gone by since Butler's visit, I went back to Karrol Maughmer for help. She informed the Lieutenant Governor's office and the State Controller's office of our story, and we were quickly put on the November calendar. Phone calls from various parties in Sacramento assured us that our proposal would go through without a further hitch. Then we received a notice that a meeting was scheduled for December 4 in Sacramento. The notice recommended that the State accept $500 from us as a settlement of their royalty claim. Even Gary re-surfaced to attend the meeting.

But the State had not given up its flair for the dramatic. We were told that the meeting had been called off. Then it was on again, and off, then on again—but the last notice arrived too late to enable us to get there in time. When we finally arrived the meeting hall was empty.

We suspected that we might have been deliberately excluded from the meeting. Had they been afraid we would make a speech, or bring the press with us, or create some sort of disturbance?

We rushed to the Controller's office. The secretary said she thought our proposal had gone through.

After lunch we went to the State Lands Commission for confirmation. The secretary sent out Willard, who had been at the second San Francisco meeting. We asked him about the settlement and he confirmed that it had gone through. He said that when he got back to Los Angeles he would write an official document and send it to us so that we could send our settlement check. That was all there was to it!

Jim dropped a verbal bomb. "How can we file papers for a prospecting permit to collect jade at Jade Cove?"

Willard was shocked. "You really know how to hurt a guy, don't you?"

We laughed nervously. It had been a legitimate question.

"We thought all that was settled, and now you guys want to continue with it."

Willard seemed confused by our presence, as though the State had chopped us up and buried our bodies in a far corner of a garden where we were to be forgotten, but here we were alive and all back together again. Willard said we would have to write a letter stating our intentions, etc., but he doubted that it would go through.

I tried to explain our intentions, "All we really want to do is to lift a few rocks so we can make a movie. Nothing too big—maybe 1,000 pounds or so."

Jim added quickly, "Of course, once we've raised them we have to take them."

Back home we waited impatiently for the settlement papers. Finally, I mailed a $500 check to the State Lands Commission stating that in cashing the check the State would not imply our guilt in any manner but would indicate that full settlement of the disputed claim had been agreed to by the State, giving us clear title to the *Nephripod*.

35. SLEEPING DRAGONS

ON JANUARY 11, 1973, one-and-a-half years after we had floated the *Nephripod* ashore at Willow Creek, we received clear title papers to it, stamped with the official State seal. Now it was over.

The past years and their images well up in my mind like an emerging kaleidoscope of ocean landscapes. Images materialize: our dream to take a rock, the equipment, the four of us stepping out of time on that mystic and primitive coast, the "bunny walk," the sea, Tarkin, Hank, and the other people, Indians, the jade canoe, pirates real and imagined, Ernie, the magic of the rock. Then our sudden victory, and back to the now-world of cities and civilization, to the Chinatown people-celebration of acceptance and understanding, to the new magic of voices at a rock show. Then the wall thrown up by the State, as unbelievable to us as a wall materialized by a wicked witch in a childhood fairy tale. Then suddenly, our unforeseen rescue by the good queen of the South, in the guise of Karrol Maughmer, "concerned citizen." And so we live happily ever after.

But ours is a true story and true stories aren't supposed to end like that. Whether it is real or imagined, the pieces fit together for me as though it *had* to happen the way it did. But I can speak only for myself, not for the others, for our group has scattered. I haven't heard from Sonny, other than to learn that his airplane was totally demolished in an accident from which he survived unscathed. Gary, having acquired enough money to last him for a while, is in Europe skiing with his ballet dancer. Jim sold his San Francisco house and bought another, which he is remodeling. He wants to go back to the Cove and muck around with history, gold mines, and old timers. I wouldn't mind joining him, but I am committed to this story and to the completion of my academic research. After that, I want to go somewhere to dive and do some thinking.

In the isolation of my garage the *Nephripod* waits with timeless patience to come to life again beneath the gentle hands of people. It can wait for our dream to see it in a public place. It has now been immortalized in the *Guinness Book of World Records* as the largest precious stone, a submarine boulder of jade weighing five tons (only 1,000 pounds off), and valued at $180,000.

Perhaps I rubbed the *Nephripod* too long. As Tarkin said, "Things go on around it." It is as though I had held a piece of life up to the sunlight—*my* life—and in it had seen vague images of certain needs and dreams. I had taken these images and transformed them into a primitive adventure and then had been allowed to bring them back whole, and somehow changed, from another world.

The State's action was the only jarring note. The message that came through is a beacon—as real as the beacon light on Cape San Martin—to all who dare to step out of the mold and become voyagers. The message is a warning of a system which has become too big and ponderous, too dehumanized to relate to human beings. Through the filtered light of bureaucratic tangle and legal jargon, the truth and nobility of our own slain dragon symbolically turns ugly. The *Nephripod* had washed up like rotting flesh upon the asphalt shore of people who did not understand.

To me, seeking my truth beyond tangible reality, the *Nephripod*, which in the final analysis both conquered me and freed me, is a sign I cannot ignore. It had helped me to move at last out of a dream into a deeper reality of life. Now, like Joyce's Stephan Dedalus, I see the world with a new perception.

Our adventure with the *Nephripod* was undertaken, then, not "because it was there" but because of certain needs within each of us. But man is restless: tomorrow life begins anew, and at the next tide we discover that the beach has changed its conformation. The incurable romantic naively steps out into the sunlight once more and, like Don Quixote, eyes another windmill, fully convinced that he has learned more and is truer, wiser, and better for his past experience.

Jade Cove seems very remote now. Someday, and soon, I will again descend the narrow switchback trail to the base of the cliff, swim through the jade cave in the CaveRock and across the Gravel Pit to visit the place where the *Nephripod* once lay.□

APPENDIX

NOTES ON COASTAL GEOLOGY AND HISTORY OF JADE

EVEN the casual tourist is curiously drawn to the Big Sur coast, where the awesome landscape is a tangle of geological confusion and mystery. Jagged and worn shore-rocks point abruptly skyward from the sea in mute ageless protest. They are etched with strata lines that tilt at crazy angles, fold back on themselves, or shear off blankly to continue a few feet or many miles away. Ancient marine terraces are perched high above the sea. Rock islands jut suddenly out of mountain meadow landscapes. Volcanic rock is interspersed with sedimentary material. The land is crossed with fault lines of international reputation, where slippage causes yearly tremors.

Geological theory offers an explanation for this precarious and jumbled landscape. Two hundred million years ago all the continents of the earth were bound together into one vast supercontinent. This supercontinent broke into many large segments, or plates, which, floating on the dense and viscous material of the earth's mantle, drifted apart and eventually formed the continents that we know today. The earth's outer crust is composed of many such plates, which are of comparatively low density and are from 10 to 40 miles thick. The thicker plates form the continents and the thinner plates are beneath the oceans.

From 45 to 150 million years ago the North American continental plate was still drifting slowly westward relative to the mid-Atlantic. In the same time span, far off the Pacific coast, basaltic lava from the interior of the earth welled up intermittently along a submerged welt, or "ridge" and spewed out new oceanic crust, forcing a spreading of the Pacific Ocean floor both to the west and to the east. The plate of the eastern Pacific floor was gradually forced against the thicker continental plate and descended beneath the edge of the North American continent. At this zone of conflict a huge trench formed, into which slid eroded sedimentary land components and even torn-off blocks of continental material.

Over a period of time, some 20 to 30 million years ago, this accumulation of trench debris containing oceanic crust and mantle, deep water and continental sedimentary material, collided with, encroached on, and destroyed the continental margin. It also became subject to compressional uplifting, sinking, folding, and slipping. These dramatic, but slowly evolving events, finally lifted much of this melange of trench material out of the sea to form the twisted and confused strata of what is now the Coast Ranges of California.

It is speculated that 30 million years ago these ranges originated far to the south of their present location, their original formation taking place off of what is now Baja California in Mexico. Since then they have moved northward as much as 650 miles. The Coast Ranges are still shifting along the San Andreas Fault and other lesser-known faults, moving northwestward in the general direction of the Aleutian Islands.

At the present time the ancient (and dormant?) marine trench is gone, and the western edge of the North American continent, partly submerged beneath the Pacific Ocean, still continues to rise.

But where did the jade come from? Again looking back about 150 million years, one theory envisions the ancestral mineral which was to become Monterey jade starting on a long journey through the ages. Through space, the journey was long too, perhaps beginning as far to the west as the longitude of the Hawaiian Islands. This ancestral jade was located not only beneath the ocean but as far as 60 miles below the earth's crust, in the viscous upper mantle at temperatures in excess of $1200°C$. It was a dense mineral known as *peridotite*, consisting largely of magnesium-rich silicates. Some geologists think that the peridotite migrated slowly shoreward with the eastern Pacific plate, until it was thrust down in the trench and then pushed up against the edge of the North American continent. During its long journey eastward it rose and cooled and when it approached the surface, having originated under high pressure and at high temperature, it was out of equilibrium and therefore unstable. Water from continental sediments and ocean seepage hydrated the peridotite rapidly and changed it to *serpentine*. When it became serpentinized, things happened to it. As water was taken in calcium was released and, since it could not be reincorporated into the serpentine, it had no place to go. Associated waters thus became calcium-saturated and filtered through the large masses of serpentine to the outer edges, where the serpentine was in contact with other minerals. At these contact points, over a long period of time and with a certain amount of pressure and heat, there was sometimes a very strong reaction within the serpentine. From this reaction the *nephrite jade* was formed, incorporating the calcium.

Although little is known about the actual mechanical changes that took place to form *Monterey jade*, replacement of certain chemicals in the lenses of rock which became jade are explained by an ion migration

to more stable assemblages under conditions of stress and temperature. The controlling factor was the composition of the migrating pore
solutions, especially the concentration of iron and calcium, depending
upon what was available from the surrounding minerals.

Pore solutions from the surrounding environment both form jade and
give it color. Pure jade is white, while colored jade results from traces of
impurities. The bright imperial green in Burmese jade is imparted by
iron, an introduced impurity.

There is a certain sadness to being such latecomers to the earth, to
having such a short view of time in either direction and so little
understanding of the earth's processes. On a cliff 180 feet above Jade
Cove I have dug out small surf-rounded pebbles from the meadow
beneath my feet. This very meadow, with its fertile brown soil, now
called a marine terrace, was once a beach so ancient that no person
ever walked its shores. The jade pebbles I now pick up were torn from
matrix materials in that far off time, rounded by an ancient sea, then
thrown onto the shore to be lifted slowly with the rest of the terrace to
their present position.

Such geological changes are not over. Sensitive modern instruments
can feel the almost daily shifting of the earth's underpinnings along fault
lines, and the Coast Ranges still rise, slip, and erode. The jade I now find
high on the cliff is also still in the process of geological change. While
now completely formed and safe from the rapid wearing action of the
sea, this jade is still being stained by the intrusion of pore materials
which seep into it from the soil or shale of its "recent" displacement and
color it red or yellow. (A beautiful example of such coloring is in a three-
pound rock owned by Jim Norton. When the end was cut off the rock, a
cross-section showed a bright gold-yellow wreath surrounding the
rock's deep blue-green core. The gold-yellow coloring was probably still
in the process of penetrating to the heart of the jade when it was dug up
from the cliffside less than twenty years ago.) Perhaps, even at this time,
jade is in the process of being created far beneath the Cove's crust,
where heat, pressure, and geological time still hide.

The history of jade, both in China and in the New World, is as
shrouded in speculation as is the origin of the mineral. And that seems
as it should be. Richard Gump, in his book *Jade: Stone of Heaven*, has
a moving passage in his first chapter, "What is Jade?":

"Jade is no ordinary stone.
Not even an ordinary 'precious' stone.

It has a 'certain something' that made a Chinese emperor offer fifteen cities for a jade carving he could hold in one hand; that made Montezuma smile when he heard that Cortez was interested only in gold, since Montezuma's most precious possession was jade. That caused men of civilizations oceans and centuries apart to believe it to be the 'stone of immortality.' That made some men forbid it to their wives, and other men to speak through it to their gods, and still others spend years carving a single object from it.

For there is a magic about jade that seems to elude man's definition, that sets it apart from all other stones. A mystery that lies beyond man's appreciation of its rarity or the skillful carving of its surface; that entices and comes closest to revealing itself when man handles 'the stone of Heaven.' A special, hidden beauty that causes men, when they speak of jade, to speak in the language of myth and legend—ordinary words are limited; the special quality within the jade stone is not."

The use of jade in China is at least as old as recorded history, and perhaps goes back to an early "stone age" when the Chinese fashioned simple implements and weapons out of jade—probably before 2000 B.C. Since that time, it has never been out of vogue with the Chinese. To the ancient Chinese, as well as to the Aztecs, jade was more valued than gold, for in athletic contests, and later as a reward for scholarship, the first prize was always jade, whereas the second was gold, and the third ivory.

There is no proof that jade was found in its raw state in China, although some scholars suspect that it was in very ancient times and that the mines were exhausted. Before the mid-18th century the Chinese got their raw jade—which was nephrite jade—from Chinese Turkestan. In 1784, when a treaty ended hostilities between China and Burma, the resumption of trade brought a different type of jade that the Chinese had not seen before. Now called *jadeite,* it is highly valued for its bright green and purity of color. When jadeite first appeared in China the Chinese did not accept it as "true" jade. To them nephrite was still the "stone of Heaven," the gem of mythology and symbolism, and the new stone was merely the "stone of Burma." Surely the different properties of the two minerals must have been detected by those who carved and worked with them, but the stones were not recognized as two different minerals.

Because nephrite was considered the "real" jade, and the jade at Jade Cove is nephrite, we can smugly accept it as being better because it has a longer history of use by man. However, although it is a Johnny-come-lately, we cannot close our eyes to the fact that Burmese and other jadeite often has brighter and more vivid color and is usually more translucent, or to the fact that it eventually became the more sought-after of the two.*

Many cultures have prized jade throughout the ages: the Chinese, the Maoris of New Zealand, the Aztecs, the Mayas, the Eskimos, the northwest Indians of America, and many peoples of the Near East. In recent times, jade has become valued worldwide. Many ancient and primitive civilizations prized jade in minor ways. Judging from artifacts found in the shell mounds around Jade Cove, I believe that the local Indians had a special regard for it, using jade pebbles for tools and possibly charms, although they did not carve it because of its hardness.

The written history of Monterey jade began in 1935, when Spencer Parmalee sent a beach-worn pebble to Stanford University for identification. However, local people may have collected jade long before 1935. A booklet entitled *Jade in California,* published in Sausalito, states:

> "Legend has it that in 1880 a fur hunter, harvesting sea lions along the steep cliffs of this wild country [sea lions still bask in the sun along the Monterey coast], pursued his quarry into a shallow green cave. He took home a few pebbles from the cave, and for two generations they were family 'keepsakes,' though they were not recognized as jade for half a century."

That Chinese gold miners were also silently picking up jade in the 1800's is proven by some of the old gold claims in Placer County, California, where jadeite rocks are found in gold tailings in all but the claims that were worked by the Chinese. By the mid-1800's many of these Chinese miners, forced out of the Sierra gold mining country, migrated to the Santa Lucia Mountains of Monterey County to dig in tougher, less known, and less lucrative gold country. It would be difficult to imagine that the Chinese miners who worked near Jade Cove remained unaware of the local jade deposits.

Nephrite and *jadeite* are two different minerals, but they are commonly indistinguishable from each other. Some pieces even confuse experts. The chemical composition is different. *Nephrite,* an amphibole, a compact fibrous variety between actinolite and tremolite, has the chemical formula $Ca(Mg,Fe)_3(SiO_3)_4$. *Jadeite,* a pyroxene $Na_2O \cdot Al_2O_3 4SiO_2$, is a silicate of sodium and aluminum. *Nephrite* is considered the most durable of rocks, due to the fibrous, asbestoslike microstructure of its crystals. However, it is 6 to 6½ on Moh's scale, not as hard as *jadeite. Jadeite* with a crystalline structure, is 6½ to 7 on Moh's scale.